heavenly
chocolate

heavenly
chocolate

divinely decadent: the ultimate cookbook

christine france

southwater

This edition is published by Southwater

Southwater is an imprint of Anness Publishing Ltd
Hermes House, 88–89 Blackfriars Road, London SE1 8HA
tel. 020 7401 2077; fax 020 7633 9499
www.southwaterbooks.com; info@anness.com

This edition distributed in the UK by The Manning Partnership Ltd
6 The Old Dairy, Melcombe Road, Bath BA2 3LR; tel. 01225 478 444; fax 01225 478 440
sales@manning-partnership.co.uk

This edition distributed in the USA and Canada by National Book Network, 4720 Boston Way
Lanham, MD 20706; tel. 301 459 3366; fax 301 459 1705; www.nbnbooks.com

This edition distributed in Australia by Pan Macmillan Australia, Level 18, St Martins Tower
31 Market St, Sydney, NSW 2000; tel. 1300 135 113; fax 1300 135 103
email customer.service@macmillan.com.au

This edition distributed in New Zealand by The Five Mile Press (NZ) Ltd
PO Box 33–1071 Takapuna, Unit 11/101–111 Diana Drive, Glenfield, Auckland 10
tel. (09) 444 4144; fax (09) 444 4518; fivemilenz@clear.net.nz

Publisher: Joanna Lorenz
Managing Editor: Linda Fraser
Food Editor: Rosemary Wilkinson
Copy Editor: Jenni Fleetwood
Designer: Annie Moss
Mac Artist: John Fowler
Photography: Steve Baxter
Food for Photography: Jane Stevenson
Styling: Diana Civil

Previously published as *Chocolate Ecstasy*

1 3 5 7 9 10 8 6 4 2

NOTES

Standard spoon and cup measures are level.

Large eggs are used unless otherwise stated.

CONTENTS

$\mathcal{I}$NTRODUCTION

Few foods are as rich, sensuous and wickedly tempting as chocolate. Whether you nibble it, savor it or simply surrender to its charms, chocolate is pure pleasure. There's something almost addictive about this gift of the gods, as anyone who has ever tried to give it up, however briefly, will testify.

The ultimate decadent treat, it is hardly surprising that in the past chocolate has been credited with being an aphrodisiac. Chocolates are traditional lovers' gifts, and special events, such as Easter and Christmas, are celebrated with chocolate eggs or the traditional yuletide log.

Once the preserve of Aztec emperors, highly prized and coveted, chocolate was unknown in Europe until the middle of the 16th century, when it was introduced as a rare and wonderful beverage. It took almost two hundred years before the sweetened chocolate bar made its appearance, and the rest, as they say, is history. Although chocolate is now accessible to all, familiarity has done nothing to dim its popularity. Consumption of all types of chocolate continues to rise. In recent years there has been an increased demand for the pure product with more than 50 percent cocoa solids, and foodies scout out new varieties of chocolate with all the enthusiasm and energy of the ardent wine buff or truffle fancier.

For the cook, the fascination with chocolate goes even deeper. It is a sensitive ingredient which needs careful handling, but which offers remarkable rewards. The velvety texture and rich flavor add a touch of luxury to numerous cakes, cookies, puddings and desserts, and chocolate is equally good in hot or cold dishes.

As an added bonus, chocolate can be piped, shaped and molded to make a variety of exciting decorations. Full instructions, with detailed advice on a range of other techniques, are included in the introduction.

This is a book for serious chocolate lovers. As you would expect, we've included classics like Black Forest Cake and Mississippi Mud Pie, but – and this is the mark of the true chocoholic – we've also investigated every conceivable way of introducing our favorite ingredient into familiar and much-loved dishes. There's a rich chocolate trifle, a rare chocolate pavlova (with cocoa giving the

meringue a dusky appearance and delectable flavor), an unusual chocolate crème brulée, a chocolate zabaglione and even a chocolate and cherry polenta cake with an unusual nutty texture.

Basic advice includes instructions for making chocolate pastry, and for those who really don't believe you can get too much of a good thing, there are double delights like Tiramisu in Chocolate Cups, White Chocolate Vanilla Mousse with Dark Chocolate Sauce and Steamed Chocolate and Fruit Puddings with Chocolate Syrup.

Also in the luscious line-up are crunchy chocolate chip cookies, chocolate sponge cakes with fudgy centers, gloriously gooey puddings, voluptuous cakes and sweet chocolate treats for gifts and after-dinner delights. In honor of those ancient Aztecs, there's a recipe for Mexican Hot Chocolate and even an iced chocolate and peppermint drink.

So go on – indulge yourself. But take it slow and easy – Death by Chocolate could be just around the corner!

TYPES OF CHOCOLATE

COUVERTURE

The professionals' choice, this is a fine quality pure chocolate with a high percentage of cocoa butter, which gives it a high gloss. It is suitable for decorative use and for making handmade chocolates. Couverture is expensive and must generally be tempered before use (see page 13). Specialty baking stores sell couverture chocolate.

DARK CHOCOLATE

Often called semisweet, bittersweet or European-style chocolate, this has a high percentage of cocoa solids – around 75 percent – slightly sweetened with sugar. The terms are often used interchangeably, but semisweet is generally sweeter than bittersweet. The rich, intense flavor and deep color make it ideal for desserts and cakes.

UNSWEETENED CHOCOLATE

Unsweetened chocolate is the most widely available chocolate to use in cooking. It contains anywhere between 30 percent and 70 percent cocoa solids, so check the label before you buy. The higher the cocoa solids, the better the chocolate flavor will be.

MILK CHOCOLATE

This contains milk and generally has around 20 percent cocoa solids. The flavor is mild and sweet. The most popular eating chocolate, it is not as suitable as unsweetened for melting and cooking.

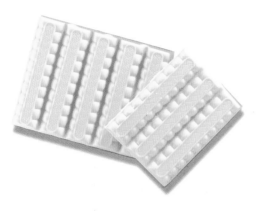

WHITE CHOCOLATE
This does not contain any cocoa solids, and gets its flavor from cocoa butter. It is sweet, and better-quality white chocolate is quite rich and smooth. White chocolate must be melted with care, since it does not withstand heat as well as regular chocolate and is liable to stiffen if allowed to get too hot.

CHOCOLATE CHIPS
These are small pieces of chocolate of uniform size, convenient for stirring directly into cookie dough or cake batter, or for melting. They contain fewer cocoa solids than ordinary chocolate, and are available in semisweet, milk and white.

UNSWEETENED COCOA
This is made from the pure cocoa solids after most of the cocoa butter has been extracted. The mass is roasted, then ground to make a powder. It is probably the most economical way of giving baked goods and puddings a chocolate flavor.

ORGANIC CHOCOLATE
This is slightly more expensive than other types of chocolate but is a quality product, high in cocoa solids, produced without pesticides and with consideration for the environment. Dark, milk and flavored varieties are available.

SWEET CHOCOLATE
This is a blend of sugar, vegetable oil, cocoa and flavorings. As its name suggests, it should be used only for covering or decoration, since it doesn't taste very good. However, the high fat content makes it suitable for making chocolate curls or caraque – to improve the flavor, melt a few squares with good unsweetened chocolate.

TECHNIQUES

Melting Chocolate

There are basically three ways to melt chocolate:

USING A DOUBLE BOILER

1 Fill the bottom of a double boiler or saucepan about a quarter full with water. Place the top pan or a heat proof bowl over the saucepan. The water should not touch the top container. Bring the water to just below the boiling point, then turn down the heat to the lowest possible setting.

2 Break the chocolate into squares and place in the top pan or bowl. Let the chocolate melt completely, without stirring. Keep the water at a very low simmer.

TIPS FOR MELTING CHOCOLATE

• Melt chocolate slowly, as overheating will spoil both the flavor and texture.
• Avoid overheating – dark chocolate should not be heated above 120°F; milk and white chocolate should not go above 110°F.
• Never allow water or steam to come into contact with melting chocolate, as this may cause it to stiffen.
• Do not cover chocolate after melting, as condensation could cause it to stiffen.

MELTING IN THE MICROWAVE

Break the chocolate into squares and place it in a bowl suitable for use in the microwave. Heat until just softened – chocolate burns easily in the microwave, so check often, remembering that chocolate retains its shape when melted in this way.

Approximate times for melting unsweetened or milk chocolate in a 650–700 watt microwave:

4 ounces	2 minutes on high (100% power)
7-8 ounces	3 minutes on high (100% power)
4 ounces white chocolate	2 minutes on medium (50% power)

DIRECT HEAT METHOD

This method is suitable only when the chocolate is to be melted in liquid, such as milk or cream. Break up the chocolate into a saucepan. Add the liquid, then heat gently, stirring occasionally, until the chocolate has melted and the mixture is smooth.

Storing Chocolate

Chocolate keeps well if stored in a cool, dry place, away from strong smelling foods. Check "best before" dates on the pack.

Tempering Chocolate

Couverture (pure chocolate with no fats other than cocoa butter) must be tempered before use. The process distributes the cocoa fat evenly and produces a glossy finish. Use for special decorations or molded chocolates.

1 Break up the chocolate into small pieces and place it in the top of a double boiler or a heat proof bowl over a saucepan of hot water. Heat gently until just melted.

2 Pour about three-quarters of the chocolate onto a marble slab or a cool, smooth work surface.

3 With a flexible plastic spatula or metal frosting knife, spread the chocolate thinly, then scoop it up, keeping it constantly on the move, for about 5 minutes.

4 Using a candy thermometer, check the temperature of the chocolate as you work it. As soon as the temperature registers 82°F, pour the chocolate back into the bowl and stir into the remaining chocolate.

5 With the addition of the hot chocolate, the temperature should now be 90°F, and the chocolate is ready for use. To test, drop a little of the chocolate from a spoon onto the marble; it should set very quickly.

Chocolate Decorations

All these decorations can be made using dark, milk or white chocolate.

GRATED CHOCOLATE

Using a fine or coarse cheese grater or the grating blade of a food processor, grate a large bar of chocolate. Grated chocolate is useful for sprinkling over desserts or cakes, or coating the sides of tortes. If you use a box cheese grater, stand it on a sheet of baking parchment or waxed paper for added convenience. The grated chocolate can then be brushed off easily as required.

QUICK CHOCOLATE CURLS

Use a bladed vegetable peeler to shave curls of chocolate from the whole bar. This process works best when the chocolate has been brought to room temperature.

CHOCOLATE CURLS

This method makes larger chocolate curls.

1 Spread melted chocolate thinly and evenly over a marble slab or a cool, smooth work surface. Let sit until the chocolate is just set.

2 Push a sharp knife or cheese slicer across the surface, at a 25-degree angle, to remove thin shavings of chocolate which should curl gently against the blade. If the chocolate sets too hard it may become too brittle to curl and must be gently melted again.

CARAQUE

This method makes beautiful, long, curled shavings which are a really special decoration for tortes and desserts. For a marbled caraque, spread out dark and white chocolate in stripes.

1 Spread melted chocolate thinly and evenly over a marble slab or a cool, smooth work surface. Let sit until the chocolate is just set.

2 Using a cook's knife with a straight, rigid blade, pull the blade across the surface of the chocolate at an angle of about 45 degrees, to remove fine, curled shavings.

PIPED SHAPES

Use your imagination when piping shapes, from simple swirls or zigzags to intricate flowers or initials, to decorate that special cake.

1 Spoon about 1 tablespoon of melted chocolate into a small paper piping bag. Fold over and secure the top, then snip a small piece off the tip of the bag with scissors.

2 Spread a sheet of parchment paper on a cool, smooth work surface or inverted baking sheet. Draw shapes on the paper as a guide if you like, or work freehand.

3 Leave the outlines as they are or fill them in to make solid decorations (a contrasting color of chocolate looks very impressive). Leave until set before carefully lifting the shapes off the paper.

4 To make curved shapes, place the paper over a rolling pin or similar shape when drying the chocolate.

CUT-OUTS

Simple cut-out shapes are a useful decoration for all kinds of cakes and desserts. Dark and white chocolate can be marbled together for a special effect.

1 Melt the chocolate and spread it on a sheet of waxed paper. Let sit until the chocolate is just set.

2 Use a sharp knife to cut triangles or squares from the chocolate, or stamp out decorative shapes, such as hearts and flowers.

CHOCOLATE LEAVES

Use any non-poisonous fresh leaves, such as rose, mint, bay, strawberry or lemon geranium. The leaves should be clean, dry and unblemished. Use both dark and white chocolate to make variegated leaves.

1 Melt the chocolate and use a small paintbrush to paint over the underside of each leaf, just up to the edges. The chocolate coating should be even and not too thin, or it will crack when you remove it.

2 Lay the leaves, chocolate side up, on a sheet of waxed paper and chill until completely set.

3 When the chocolate has set, carefully peel away the leaves to reveal the veined chocolate leaves. If necessary, pack into airtight containers and store in a cool place.

FEATHERED OR MARBLED CHOCOLATE

These two related techniques provide some of the easiest and most effective ways of decorating the top of a cake, and can also be used for making swirled or marble cut-outs. Chocolate sauce and cream frostings can also be feathered or marbled to decorate a dessert.

1 Melt two contrasting colors of chocolate and spread one over the cake or surface to be decorated.

2 Spoon the contrasting chocolate into a piping bag and pipe lines or swirls over the chocolate.

3 Working quickly, before the chocolate sets, draw a skewer or toothpick through the swirls to create a feathered or marbled effect.

CHOCOLATE RIBBONS

These look particularly striking if dark and white chocolate are used to make striped or dotted ribbons.

1 Cut strips of clear acetate into long, thin strips, about 6 x 2 inches.

2 Melt the chocolate and spoon into piping bags. Pipe the chocolate in your chosen design over the strips, making a straight edge. Use a ruler to guide your hand in a straight line.

3 Allow to cool until it holds its shape but do not allow it to set. Bend each ribbon over with the plastic strip and secure with tape. Let sit until completely set, then peel away the plastic.

EQUIPMENT

Working with chocolate requires little by way of special equipment. Most items will be found in any well-stocked kitchen, but you may need to buy one or two extra pieces of equipment if you plan to mold chocolates.

CANDY THERMOMETER
Mainly used for tempering chocolate, or melting it for dipping.

CHEESE SLICER
The blade is drawn across a thin layer of just-set chocolate to make curls or caraque.

CHOCOLATE MOLDS
Most small chocolate molds are made from flexible plastic, though some larger ones, such as Easter egg molds, are made from polished metal.

CHOCOLATE TOOLS
Professionals use these for dipping and marking chocolates. Buy them from cake decorating suppliers.

COOKIE CUTTERS
Small cookie cutters are handy for making decorative shapes from thin sheets of set chocolate.

DOUBLE BOILER
This is useful for melting chocolate over simmering water, but a heat proof bowl fitted over an ordinary saucepan can be used instead, if done carefully.

FLEXIBLE SCRAPER
This is an asset when making chocolate caraque and shavings.

KNIVES
Small sharp knives are required for cutting chocolate shapes, while a large cook's knife with a rigid non-serrated blade is necessary for making caraque.

MARBLE SLAB
Although not essential, this provides a cold, flat surface for spreading chocolate to make shapes and is also used when tempering chocolate. A clean work surface or an inverted baking sheet can be used instead.

METAL FROSTING KNIFE
This is the perfect tool for spreading melted chocolate or frostings.

MIXING BOWLS
A selection of mixing bowls in various sizes is essential. Heat proof bowls are necessary for melting chocolate, and a large glass or ceramic bowl will be invaluable for whisking egg whites.

PAINTBRUSHES
Small paintbrushes can be used for spreading chocolate thinly over leaves or inside molds. Choose good-quality brushes that will not shed hairs.

SIEVE
A standard sieve is needed for sifting cocoa and confectioners' sugar. For very small quantities, use a tea strainer.

TOOTHPICKS AND SKEWERS
These are useful for marbling chocolate and moving delicate shapes such as caraque or curls.

VEGETABLE PEELER
Use this for making chocolate curls.

1 DOUBLE BOILER

2 KNIFE

3 METAL FROSTING KNIFE

4 FLEXIBLE SCRAPER

5 CHEESE SLICER

6 VEGETABLE PEELER

7 CHOCOLATE TOOLS

8 CANDY
THERMOMETER

9 PAINTBRUSHES

10 TOOTHPICKS
AND SKEWERS

11 CHOCOLATE MOLDS

12 COOKIE CUTTERS

13 SIEVE

14 MIXING BOWLS

15 MARBLE SLAB

$\mathcal{S}$MALL CAKES AND TREATS

There's no end to the ways to use chocolate in small cakes and cookies. Start the day with a warm Brioche au Chocolat for breakfast, or treat yourself at coffee time with rich, totally indulgent Nut and Chocolate Chip Brownies or Double Chocolate Chip Muffins. Or, if you're after an elegant touch of texture to serve alongside a creamy dinner party dessert, light, crisp Chocolate Cinnamon Tuiles are the perfect choice.

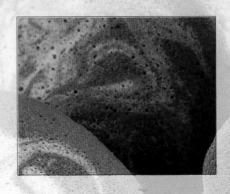

Nut and Chocolate Chip Brownies

INGREDIENTS

5 ounces unsweetened baking
chocolate, broken into squares

½ cup sunflower oil

1¼ cups light brown sugar

2 eggs

1 teaspoon vanilla extract

⅔ cup self-rising flour

4 tablespoons unsweetened cocoa

¾ cup chopped walnuts
or pecans

4 tablespoons milk chocolate chips

≈ MAKES 16 ≈

*Moist, dark and deeply satisfying –
meet the ultimate chocolate brownie.*

1 Preheat the oven to 350°F.
Lightly grease a shallow
8-inch square baking pan. Melt
the unsweetened chocolate in a
heat proof bowl over hot
water.

COOK'S TIP

*These brownies will
freeze for 3 months in an
airtight container*

2 Beat the oil, sugar, eggs
and vanilla extract together
in a large bowl.

3 Stir in the melted
chocolate, then beat well
until evenly mixed.

4 Sift the flour and cocoa
powder into the bowl and
fold in thoroughly.

5 Stir in the chopped nuts
and chocolate chips, pour
into the prepared pan and
spread evenly to the edges.

6 Bake for 30-35 minutes,
or until a thin crust has
formed on top. Cool in the
pan before cutting the
brownies into squares.

WHITE CHOCOLATE MACADAMIA SLICES

Keep these luxurious slices for someone who'll really appreciate their rich flavor and superb texture.

3 In the top of a double boiler or heat proof bowl set over barely simmering water, melt the remaining white chocolate with the butter. Remove from the heat and stir in the vanilla extract.

4 Whisk the eggs and sugar together in a mixing bowl until thick and pale, then pour in the melted chocolate mixture, whisking constantly.

1 Preheat the oven to 375°F. Lightly grease two 8-inch round layer cake pans and line the base of each with a circle of baking parchment or wax paper cut to fit neatly.

2 Roughly chop the nuts and half the white chocolate, making sure that the pieces are more or less the same size, then cut up the apricots to similar-size pieces.

5 Sift the flour over the mixture and fold it in evenly. Finally, stir in the nuts, chopped white chocolate and chopped dried apricots.

6 Spoon into the pan and level the top. Bake for 30-35 minutes, or until a thin crust has formed. Cool in the pan before cutting into squares.

COOK'S TIP

Use kitchen scissors to snip the apricots into small pieces.

CHOCOLATE CINNAMON TUILES

Slim, curvy and quite irresistible, tuiles are the perfect accompaniment for sophisticated desserts.

INGREDIENTS

1 egg white

¼ cup superfine sugar

2 tablespoons all-purpose flour

3 tablespoons butter, melted

1 tablespoon unsweetened cocoa

½ teaspoon ground cinnamon

~ MAKES 12 ~

1 Preheat the oven to 400°F. Lightly grease two large baking sheets. Whisk the egg white in a clean, grease-free bowl until it forms soft peaks. Gradually whisk in the sugar to make a smooth, glossy mixture.

COOK'S TIP

Work as quickly as possible when removing the tuiles from the baking sheets – if they harden too quickly, pop the baking sheet back in the oven for a minute and try again.

2 Sift the flour over the mixture and fold in evenly. Stir in the butter. Transfer about 3 tablespoons of the mixture to a small bowl and set it aside.

3 In a separate bowl, stir together the cocoa and cinnamon. Stir into the larger quantity of batter.

4 Leaving room for spreading, drop spoonfuls of the chocolate-flavored mixture onto the prepared baking sheets, then spread each gently with a metal frosting knife to make a neat circle.

5 Using a small spoon, drizzle the reserved plain batter over the rounds, swirling it lightly to create an attractive marbled effect.

6 Bake for 4-6 minutes, until just set. Using a frosting knife, lift each cookie carefully and quickly drape it over a rolling pin to give it a curved shape as it hardens.

7 Allow the tuiles to cool until set, then remove them gently and finish cooling on a wire rack. Serve on the same day.

DOUBLE CHOCOLATE CHIP MUFFINS

INGREDIENTS

3½ cups all-purpose flour

1 tablespoon baking powder

2 tablespoons unsweetened cocoa

¾ cup dark brown sugar

2 eggs

⅔ cup sour cream

⅔ cup milk

4 tablespoons sunflower oil

6 ounces white chocolate

6 ounces semisweet chocolate

unsweetened cocoa, for dusting

MAKES 16

COOK'S TIP

If sour cream is not available, you can easily sour ⅔ cup cream by stirring in 1 teaspoon lemon juice and letting the mixture stand until thickened.

> *Marvellous muffins, packed with lots of chunky dark and white chocolate chips.*

1 Preheat the oven to 375°F.
~ Place 16 paper liners in muffin pans. Sift together the flour, baking powder and cocoa into a bowl and stir in the sugar to thoroughly combine the ingredients. Make a well in the center of the mixture.

2 In a separate bowl, beat the
~ eggs with the sour cream, milk and oil, then stir into the well in the dry ingredients. Beat well, gradually incorporating the flour mixture to make a thick and creamy batter.

3 Chop both the white and
~ the semisweet chocolate into small pieces, then stir into the batter.

4 Spoon the mixture into the
~ muffin cups, filling them almost to the top. Bake for 25-30 minutes, until well risen and firm to the touch. Cool on a wire rack, then dust with cocoa.

CHOCOLATE MARZIPAN COOKIES

Crisp little cookies for a sweet tooth, with a little almond surprise inside.

INGREDIENTS

14 tablespoons unsalted butter, softened

1 generous cup light brown sugar

1 egg

2¾ cups all-purpose flour

4 tablespoons unsweetened cocoa

7 ounces almond paste

4 ounces white chocolate, broken into squares

~ MAKES ABOUT 36 ~

1 Preheat the oven to 375°F. Lightly grease two large baking sheets. Cream the butter with the sugar in a bowl until pale and fluffy. Add the egg and beat well.

2 Sift the flour and cocoa over the mixture. Stir it in, first with a wooden spoon, then with clean hands, pressing the mixture together to make a fairly soft dough.

3 Roll out about half the dough on a lightly floured surface to a thickness of about ¼ inch. Using a 2-inch cookie cutter, cut out circles, re-rolling the dough as required until you have about 36 rounds.

4 Cut the almond paste into about 36 equal pieces. Roll into balls, flatten slightly and place one on each circle of dough. Roll out the remaining dough, cut out more circles, then place on top of the almond paste. Press the dough edges to seal.

5 Bake for 10–12 minutes, or until the cookies have risen and are beginning to crack on the surface. Cool on the baking sheet for about 2–3 minutes, then finish cooling on a wire rack.

6 Melt the white chocolate, then either drizzle it over the cookies to decorate, or spoon into a paper piping bag and quickly pipe a design onto the cookies.

COOK'S TIP

If the dough is too sticky to roll out, chill it for 30 minutes, then try again.

MOCHA VIENNESE SWIRLS

INGREDIENTS

4 ounces unsweetened chocolate, broken into squares

14 tablespoons unsalted butter, softened

6 tablespoons confectioners' sugar

2 tablespoons strong black coffee

1¾ cups all-purpose flour

½ cup cornstarch

To decorate

about 20 blanched almonds

5 ounces bittersweet chocolate

MAKES ABOUT 20

Some temptations just can't be resisted. Put out a plate of these melt-in-the-mouth marvels and watch them vanish.

3 Spoon the mixture into a
~ piping bag fitted with a large star tip and pipe about 20 swirls on the baking sheets, allowing room for spreading during baking.

4 Press an almond into the
~ center of each swirl. Bake for about 15 minutes or until the cookies are firm and just beginning to brown.

5 Let cool for about
~ 10 minutes on the baking sheets, then lift carefully onto a wire rack to cool completely.

6 When cool, melt the
~ chocolate and dip the base of each swirl to coat. Place on a sheet of baking parchment or wax paper and let set.

1 Preheat the oven to 375°F.
~ Lightly grease two large baking sheets. Melt the chocolate in a bowl set over hot water. Cream the butter with the confectioners' sugar in a bowl until smooth and pale. Beat in the melted chocolate, then the strong black coffee.

2 Sift the flour and
~ cornstarch over the mixture. Fold in lightly and evenly to make a soft mixture.

COOK'S TIP

If the mixture is too stiff to pipe, soften it with a little more black coffee.

CHUNKY DOUBLE CHOCOLATE COOKIES

Keep these luscious treats under lock and key unless you're feeling generous!

INGREDIENTS

½ cup unsalted butter, softened

⅔ cup light brown sugar

1 egg

1 teaspoon vanilla extract

1¼ cups self-rising flour

¾ cup rolled oats

4 ounces bittersweet chocolate, coarsely chopped

4 ounces white chocolate, coarsely chopped

MAKES 18–20

3 Drop 18–20 generously rounded tablespoonfuls onto the baking sheets, leaving space for spreading.

4 Bake for 12–15 minutes, or until the cookies are beginning to turn a light golden brown. Cool for about 2–3 minutes on the baking sheets, then cool on wire racks.

1 Preheat the oven to 375°F. Lightly grease two baking sheets. In a large mixing bowl, cream the butter with the sugar until pale and fluffy. Add the egg and vanilla extract and beat well.

2 Sift the flour over the mixture and fold in lightly with a metal spoon. Add the oats and chopped chocolate and stir until the chocolate is evenly distributed.

COOK'S TIP

If you're short of time when making the cookies, substitute chocolate chips for the chopped chocolate. Chopped preserved ginger would make a delicious addition as well.

CRANBERRY AND CHOCOLATE SQUARES

> *Made for each other – those are the contrasting flavors of tangy-sharp cranberries and sweet chocolate.*

INGREDIENTS

1¼ cups self-rising flour, plus extra for dusting

½ cup unsalted butter

4 tablespoons unsweetened cocoa

1¼ cups light brown sugar

2 eggs, beaten

1⅓ cups fresh or thawed frozen cranberries

For the topping

⅔ cup sour cream

6 tablespoons superfine sugar

2 tablespoons self-rising flour

4 tablespoons margarine, softened

1 egg, beaten

½ teaspoon vanilla extract

5 tablespoons coarsely grated bittersweet chocolate, for sprinkling

~ MAKES 12 ~

2 Remove the melted
~ mixture from the heat and stir in the flour and eggs, beating until thoroughly mixed. Stir in the cranberries, then spread the mixture in the prepared pan.

1 Preheat the oven to 350°F.
~ Grease a 10-inch square cake pan and dust lightly with flour. Combine the butter, cocoa and sugar in a saucepan. Place over low heat and stir constantly until melted and smooth.

3 Make the topping: Mix all
~ the ingredients in a bowl. Beat until smooth, then spread over the base.

4 Sprinkle with the grated
~ chocolate and bake for 40-45 minutes, or until risen and firm. Cool in the pan, then cut into 12 squares.

CHOCOLATE CINNAMON DOUGHNUTS

> *Serve these light and luscious treats freshly made and just warm, so that the chocolate filling melts in your mouth.*

INGREDIENTS

5 cups bread flour

2 tablespoons unsweetened cocoa

½ teaspoon salt

1 package easy-blend dried yeast

1¼ cups hot milk

3 tablespoons butter, melted

1 egg, beaten

4 ounces bittersweet chocolate,
broken into 16 pieces

sunflower oil for deep frying

For the coating

3 tablespoons superfine sugar

1 tablespoon unsweetened cocoa

1 teaspoon ground cinnamon

MAKES 16

2 Knead the dough on a lightly floured surface for about 5 minutes, until smooth and elastic. Return to the clean bowl, cover and leave in a warm place until the dough has doubled in bulk.

3 Knead the dough lightly again, then divide into 16 pieces. Shape each into a circle, press a piece of chocolate into the center, then fold the dough over to enclose the filling, pressing firmly to make sure the edges are sealed. Reshape the doughnuts if necessary when sealed.

4 Heat the oil for deep frying to 350°F, or until a cube of dried bread browns in 30–45 seconds. Deep-fry the doughnuts in batches. As each doughnut rises and turns golden brown, turn it over carefully to cook the other side. Drain the doughnuts well on paper towels.

5 Mix the sugar, cocoa and cinnamon in a shallow bowl. Toss the doughnuts in the mixture to coat them evenly. Serve warm.

1 Sift the flour, cocoa and salt into a large bowl. Stir in the yeast. Make a well in the center and add the milk, melted butter and egg. Stir, gradually incorporating the dry ingredients to make a soft and pliable dough.

COOK'S TIP

If you are not planning to serve the doughnuts immediately, drain them on paper towels, cool completely and pack in an airtight container. To serve, place the doughnuts for a few minutes in a hot oven, then toss in the coating and serve warm.

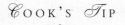

CHOCOLATE BUTTERSCOTCH BARS

INGREDIENTS

2 cups all-purpose flour

½ teaspoon baking powder

½ cup unsalted butter

⅓ cup light brown sugar

5 ounces unsweetened chocolate, melted

2 tablespoons ground almonds

For the topping

¾ cup unsalted butter

½ cup superfine sugar

2 tablespoons light corn syrup

¾ cup condensed milk

1¼ cups toasted whole hazelnuts

8 ounces semisweet chocolate, broken into squares

☞ MAKES 24 ☜

Unashamedly rich and sweet, these bars are perfect for chocoholics of all ages.

1 ~ Preheat the oven to 325°F. Lightly grease a shallow 12 x 8-inch baking pan. Sift the flour and baking powder into a large bowl.

2 ~ Rub in the butter until the mixture resembles coarse bread crumbs, then stir in the sugar. Work in the melted chocolate and almonds to make a light dough.

3 ~ Press the dough evenly into the prepared pan, prick the surface with a fork and bake for 25–30 minutes until firm. Leave to cool in the pan.

4 ~ Make the topping. Mix the butter, sugar, corn syrup and condensed milk in a pan. Heat gently, stirring, until the butter and sugar have melted. Simmer, stirring occasionally, until golden, then stir in the toasted hazelnuts.

5 ~ Pour the topping over the base and set aside.

6 ~ Melt the chocolate in a heat proof bowl over hot water. Spread evenly over the butterscotch layer, then let cool again before cutting into bars to serve.

COOK'S TIP

If you prefer to make the bars a few days before serving, bake the base on its own, and add the chocolate topping nearer serving time.

BRIOCHES AU CHOCOLAT

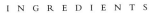

Steal out of bed early and surprise the one you love with these wonderful French specialities. Light, golden and drizzled with melted chocolate, they are bound to be a hit.

INGREDIENTS

2¼ cups bread flour

pinch of salt

2 tablespoons superfine sugar

1 packet easy-blend dried yeast

3 eggs, beaten, plus 1 beaten egg, for glazing

3 tablespoons warm milk

½ cup unsalted butter, diced

5 ounces semisweet chocolate, broken into squares

MAKES 12

1 ~ Sift the flour, salt and sugar into a large bowl and stir in the yeast. Make a well in the center of the mixture and add the eggs and milk.

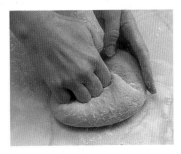

2 ~ Beat well, gradually incorporating the dry ingredients to make a fairly soft dough. Turn the dough onto a lightly floured work surface and knead until it is smooth and elastic, adding flour as necessary.

3 ~ Add the butter to the dough, a few pieces at a time, kneading until each addition is absorbed before adding the next. When all the butter has been incorporated and small bubbles appear in the dough, wrap in plastic and chill for at least 1 hour, or overnight.

4 ~ Lightly grease 12 individual brioche pans set on a baking sheet or a 12-hole brioche or muffin pan. Divide the dough into 12 pieces and shape each into a smooth circle. Place a chocolate square in the center. Bring up the sides of the dough and press the edges together to seal.

5 ~ Place the brioches, seam side down, in the prepared pans. Cover with a clean dish towel and let rise in a warm place for about 30 minutes or until doubled in bulk. Preheat the oven to 400°F.

6 ~ Brush with beaten egg; bake for 12-15 minutes, until well risen and golden brown. Place the brioches on wire racks to cool. Melt the remaining chocolate and drizzle it over the brioches.

35

LARGE CAKES, LOAVES AND PIES

There can't be many families who wouldn't leap enthusiastically at a simple chocolate cake, so think of the mouths watering at the sight of a deep, sticky slice of Chocolate Pecan Pie or Frosted Chocolate Fudge Cake. If cheesecakes are a family favorite, try Baked Chocolate and Raisin Cheesecake — so simple to make and well worth it for all the praise you'll get!

CHOCOLATE PECAN PIE

> *If you thought pecan pie couldn't be improved upon, just try this gorgeous chocolate one with its rich orange crust.*

INGREDIENTS

1¾ cups all-purpose flour

5 tablespoons superfine sugar

scant ½ cup unsalted butter, softened

1 egg, beaten

finely grated rind of 1 orange

For the filling

¾ cup light corn syrup

3 tablespoons light brown sugar

5 ounces unsweetened chocolate, broken into squares

4 tablespoons butter

3 eggs, beaten

1 teaspoon vanilla extract

1½ cups pecans

SERVES 6

1 Sift the flour into a bowl and stir in the sugar. Work in the butter evenly with the fingertips until combined.

2 Beat the egg and orange rind in a bowl, then stir into the mixture to make a firm dough. Add a little water if the mixture is too dry.

3 Roll out the pastry on a lightly floured surface and use it to line a 9-inch loose-based tart pan. Chill for 30 minutes.

4 Preheat the oven to 350°F. Make the filling. Mix the syrup, sugar, chocolate and butter in a small saucepan. Heat gently until the chocolate is melted.

5 Remove from the heat and beat in the eggs and vanilla extract. Sprinkle the pecans into the pastry shell and carefully pour in the chocolate mixture.

6 Place on a baking sheet and bake for 50-60 minutes, or until set. Cool in the pan.

COOK'S TIP

Make individual tartlets if you prefer – use six tartlet pans and bake at the same temperature for about 30 minutes. Walnuts or almonds can be used instead of pecans.

FROSTED CHOCOLATE FUDGE CAKE

> *Rich and dreamy, with an irresistible chocolate fudgy frosting, this cake couldn't be easier to make, or more wonderful to eat!*

INGREDIENTS

4 ounces unsweetened chocolate, broken into squares

¾ cup unsalted butter or margarine, softened

1 cup light brown sugar, firmly packed

1 teaspoon vanilla extract

3 eggs, beaten

⅔ cup strained plain yogurt

1¼ cups self-rising flour

confectioners' sugar and chocolate curls to decorate

For the frosting

4 ounces bittersweet chocolate, broken into squares

4 tablespoons unsalted butter

3 cups confectioners' sugar

6 tablespoons strained plain yogurt

SERVES 6–8

COOK'S TIP

If the frosting begins to set too quickly, heat it gently to soften, and beat in a little extra yogurt if necessary.

1 Preheat the oven to 375°F. Grease two 8-inch round layer cake pans and line the base of each with baking parchment or wax paper. Melt the chocolate in the top of a double boiler or a heat proof bowl placed over hot water.

2 In a mixing bowl, cream the butter or margarine with the sugar until light and fluffy. Beat in the vanilla, then gradually add the beaten eggs, beating well after each addition.

3 Stir in the melted unsweetened chocolate and yogurt evenly. Fold in the flour with a metal spoon.

4 Divide the mixture between the prepared pans. Bake for 25–30 minutes, or until the cakes are firm to the touch. Invert the cakes onto a wire rack and cool.

5 Make the frosting. Melt the chocolate and butter in a saucepan over low heat. Remove from the heat and stir in the confectioners' sugar and yogurt. Mix with a rubber spatula until smooth, then beat until the frosting begins to cool and thicken slightly. Use about a third of the mixture to sandwich the cakes together.

6 Working quickly, spread the remainder over the top and sides. Sprinkle with confectioners' sugar and decorate with chocolate curls.

Chocolate Ginger Crunch Cake

INGREDIENTS

5 ounces bittersweet chocolate, broken into squares

4 tablespoons unsalted butter

4 ounces gingersnap cookies

4 pieces preserved ginger

2 tablespoons preserved ginger syrup

3 tablespoons shredded coconut

To decorate

1 ounce milk chocolate

pieces of crystallized ginger

SERVES 6

> *Ginger adds a flicker of fire to this delectable uncooked cake. Keep one in the fridge for midnight feasts and other late-night treats.*

1 Grease a 6-inch flan ring; place it on a sheet of baking parchment. Melt the bittersweet chocolate with the butter in a heat proof bowl over barely simmering water. Remove from the heat.

3 Chop the preserved ginger fairly finely and mix with the crushed cookies.

5 Pour the mixture into the tart pan and press down firmly and evenly. Chill in the refrigerator until set.

6 Remove the bottom of the tart pan and slide the cake onto a plate. Melt the milk chocolate, drizzle it over the top and decorate with the crystallized ginger.

2 Crush the cookies into small pieces (see Cook's Tip). Place them in a bowl.

4 Stir the biscuit mixture, ginger syrup and coconut into the melted chocolate and butter, mixing well until evenly combined.

Cook's Tip

Do not crush the cookies into fine crumbs; you'll need some bigger pieces for texture. Put them in a plastic bag and crush them with a rolling pin, or chop them in a food processor, using the pulse setting for greater control.

BAKED CHOCOLATE AND RAISIN CHEESECAKE

INGREDIENTS

¾ cup all-purpose flour

3 tablespoons unsweetened cocoa

½ cup semolina

¼ cup superfine sugar

½ cup unsalted
butter, softened

For the filling

1 cup cream cheese

½ cup plain yogurt

2 eggs, beaten

6 tablespoons superfine sugar

finely grated zest of 1 lemon

½ cup raisins

¼ cup semisweet chocolate chips

For the topping

3 ounces unsweetened chocolate,
broken into squares

2 tablespoons light corn syrup

3 tablespoons butter

~ SERVES 8–10 ~

If you just can't get enough chocolate, this delectable cheesecake will be your idea of heaven. Its crisp chocolate shortbread base is covered with a creamy chocolate chip filling, topped off with a sticky chocolate glaze.

1 Preheat the oven to 300°F.
~ Sift together the flour and cocoa into a mixing bowl and stir in the semolina and sugar. Using your fingertips, work the butter into the dry ingredients until it makes a firm dough.

2 Press the dough into the
~ base of a 9-inch springform pan. Prick all over with a fork and bake in the oven for 15 minutes. Remove the pan but leave the oven on.

3 Make the filling. In a large
~ bowl, beat the cream cheese with the yogurt, eggs and sugar until evenly mixed. Stir in the lemon zest, raisins and chocolate chips.

COOK'S TIP

For a slightly quicker version, omit the topping and simply drizzle melted chocolate over the cheesecake to finish.

4 Smooth the cream cheese
~ mixture over the chocolate shortbread base and bake for 35–45 more minutes, or until the filling is pale gold and just set. Cool in the pan.

5 To make the topping,
~ combine the chocolate, syrup and butter in a heat proof bowl. Set over a saucepan of simmering water and heat gently, stirring occasionally, until melted. Pour over the cheesecake and allow to set.

CHOCOLATE CHIP MARZIPAN LOAF

INGREDIENTS

½ cup unsalted butter, softened

1 cup light brown sugar

2 eggs

3 tablespoons unsweetened cocoa

1¼ cups self-rising flour

4½ ounces marzipan

¼ cup semisweet chocolate chips

~ MAKES 1 LOAF ~

Sometimes plain wrappers disguise the most marvelous surprises. Inside this ordinary-looking loaf are creamy chunks of marzipan and chocolate.

1 Preheat the oven to 350°F. Grease a 2-pound loaf pan and line the bottom with baking parchment or wax paper. Cream the butter and sugar in a mixing bowl until light and fluffy.

2 Add the eggs to the creamed mixture one at a time, beating well after each addition to combine.

3 Sift the cocoa and flour over the mixture and fold in evenly.

4 Chop the marzipan into small pieces with a sharp knife. Place in a bowl and mix with the chocolate chips. Set aside about 4 tablespoons and fold the rest evenly into the cake mixture.

5 Scrape the mixture into the prepared pan, level the top and sprinkle with the reserved marzipan and chocolate chips.

6 Bake for 45–50 minutes or until the loaf is risen and firm. Cool for a few minutes in the pan, then turn out onto a wire rack to cool completely.

COOK'S TIP

This cake is ideal for freezing, either whole or in handy slices separated by sheets of plastic wrap. Wrap the slices in foil and freeze for up to 3 months.

$\mathscr{S}$TICKY CHOCOLATE, MAPLE AND WALNUT SWIRLS

This rich yeasted cake breaks into separate sticky chocolate swirls, each soaked in maple syrup.

INGREDIENTS

4 cups bread flour

½ teaspoon ground cinnamon

4 tablespoons unsalted butter

¼ cup superfine sugar

1 packet easy-blend dried yeast

1 egg yolk

½ cup water

4 tablespoons milk

3 tablespoons maple syrup, to finish

For the filling

3 tablespoons unsalted butter, melted

⅓ cup light brown sugar

1 cup semisweet chocolate chips

¾ cup chopped walnuts

SERVES 12

1 Grease a deep 9-inch springform pan. Sift the flour and cinnamon into a bowl, then cut in the butter until the mixture resembles coarse breadcrumbs.

2 Stir in the sugar and yeast. In a cup or bowl, beat the egg yolk with the water and milk, then stir into the dry ingredients to make a soft dough (see Cook's Tip).

3 Knead the dough on a lightly floured surface until smooth, then roll out to a rectangle measuring about 16 x 12 inches.

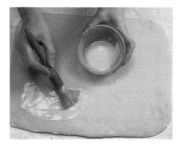

4 For the filling, brush the dough with the melted butter and sprinkle with the sugar, chocolate chips and nuts.

5 Roll up the dough from one long side like a jelly roll, then cut into 12 thick even slices.

6 Pack the slices closely together in the prepared pan, with the cut sides facing upward. Cover the dough and leave in a warm place until well risen and springy to the touch, about 1½ hours. About 15 minutes before baking, preheat the oven to 425°F.

7 Bake the swirls for about 30-35 minutes until well risen, golden brown and firm. Remove from the pan and cool on a wire rack. To finish, spoon or brush the maple syrup over the cake. Pull the pieces apart to serve.

COOK'S TIP

The amount of liquid added to the dry ingredients may have to be adjusted slightly as some flours absorb more liquid than others. The dough should be soft but not sticky.

 RANGE MARMALADE CHOCOLATE LOAF

INGREDIENTS

4 ounces unsweetened chocolate, broken into squares

3 eggs

scant 1 cup superfine sugar

¾ cup sour cream

1¾ cups self-rising flour

For the filling and glaze

⅔ cup bitter orange marmalade

4 ounces semisweet chocolate, broken into squares

4 tablespoons sour cream

shredded orange rind, to decorate

~ SERVES 8 ~

Don't be alarmed at the amount of cream in this recipe – it's naughty but necessary, and replaces butter to make a moist dark cake, topped with a bitter-sweet sticky marmalade topping.

1 Preheat the oven to 350°F. Grease a 2-pound loaf pan lightly, then line the base with a piece of baking parchment or wax paper. Melt the chocolate in a heat proof bowl placed over hot water.

2 Combine the eggs and sugar in a separate bowl. Using a hand-held electric mixer, beat the mixture until it is thick and creamy, then stir in the sour cream and chocolate. Fold in the flour evenly.

3 Pour the mixture into the prepared pan and bake for about 1 hour, or until well risen and firm to the touch. Cool for a few minutes in the pan, then turn out onto a wire rack and let the loaf cool completely.

4 Make the filling. Spoon two-thirds of the marmalade into a small saucepan and melt over low heat. Melt the chocolate and stir it into the marmalade with the sour cream.

5 Slice the cake across into three layers and sandwich back together with about half the marmalade filling. Spread the rest over the top of the cake and leave to set. Spoon the remaining marmalade over the cake and scatter with shredded orange rind, to decorate.

COOK'S TIP

If you don't particularly like marmalade, use apricot jam instead.

CHOCOLATE AND CHERRY POLENTA CAKE

INGREDIENTS

⅓ cup quick-cooking polenta

7 ounces unsweetened chocolate, broken into squares

5 eggs, separated

¾ cup superfine sugar

1 cup ground almonds

4 tablespoons all-purpose flour

finely grated zest of 1 orange

½ cup candied cherries, halved

confectioners' sugar, for dusting

— SERVES 8 —

Perfect for packing for a romantic picnic, this chocolate cherry cake is dense and delicious. Polenta and almonds add an unusual nutty texture.

1 Place the polenta in a heat proof bowl and pour over just enough boiling water to cover, about ½ cup. Stir well, then cover the bowl and leave to stand for about 30 minutes, until the polenta has absorbed all the excess moisture.

2 Preheat the oven to 375°F. Grease a deep 9-inch layer cake pan and line the base with baking parchment or wax paper. Melt the chocolate in a heat proof bowl over hot water.

3 Whisk the egg yolks with the sugar in a bowl until thick and pale. Beat in the chocolate, then fold in the polenta, ground almonds, flour and orange zest.

COOK'S TIP

It is important to add only just enough water to cover the polenta, as too much moisture in the mixture will cause the cherries to sink. If necessary, drain off excess moisture.

4 Whisk the egg whites in a clean, grease-free bowl until stiff. Stir about 1 tablespoon of the whites into the chocolate mixture to lighten it, then fold in the rest. Finally, fold in the cherries.

5 Pour the mixture into the prepared pan and bake for 45-55 minutes, or until well risen and firm to the touch. Turn out and cool on a wire rack. Dust with confectioners' sugar before serving.

MARBLED SWISS ROLL

WITH CHOCOLATE AND WALNUT BUTTERCREAM

Simply sensational – that's the combination of light chocolate sponge and walnut chocolate buttercream.

INGREDIENTS

1 tablespoon unsweetened cocoa

scant 1 cup all-purpose flour

1 ounce semisweet chocolate, grated

1 ounce white chocolate, grated

3 eggs

½ cup superfine sugar

2 tablespoons boiling water

For the filling

1 recipe Chocolate Buttercream

3 tablespoons chopped walnuts

SERVES 6–8

1 Preheat the oven to 400°F. Grease a 12 x 8-inch jelly roll pan and line it with baking parchment or wax paper. Sift the cocoa and half the flour into a large mixing bowl. Stir the grated semisweet chocolate into the flour mixture. Sift the remaining flour into another bowl; stir in the grated white chocolate.

2 Whisk the eggs and sugar in a heat proof bowl set over a pan of hot water until the mixture forms long strands when the whisk is lifted.

3 Remove the eggs from the heat and pour half the eggs into a separate bowl. Fold the white chocolate mixture into one portion, then fold the dark chocolate mixture into the other. Stir 1 tablespoon of the boiling water into each bowl to soften the batters.

4 Place alternate spoonfuls of batter in the prepared pan and swirl lightly together for a marbled effect. Bake for about 12-15 minutes, or until firm. Turn out onto a sheet of baking parchment or wax paper.

5 Trim the cake's edges to neaten and cover with a clean dish towel. Cool.

6 For the filling, mix the buttercream and walnuts in a bowl. Uncover the cake, lift off the paper and spread the surface with the buttercream. Roll up carefully from a long side and place on a serving plate. Decorate with dark and white chocolate curls, if desired.

COOK'S TIP

Use a skewer to swirl the chocolate and plain batters together. Make sure that the batter fills the corners of the pan.

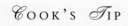

SIMPLE SCHOCOLATE CAKE

An easy, everyday chocolate cake which can be simply filled with buttercream, or pepped up with a rich chocolate ganache for a special occasion.

INGREDIENTS

4 ounces unsweetened chocolate, broken into squares

3 tablespoons milk

⅔ cup unsalted butter or margarine, softened

scant 1 cup light brown sugar

3 eggs

1¾ cups self-rising flour

1 tablespoon unsweetened cocoa

1 recipe Chocolate Buttercream, for the filling

confectioners' sugar, for dusting
unsweetened cocoa, for dusting

SERVES 6–8

1 Preheat the oven to 350°F. Grease two 7-inch round layer cake pans and line the base of each with baking parchment or wax paper. Melt the chocolate with the milk in a heat proof bowl set over a pan of simmering water.

2 Cream the butter or margarine with the sugar in a mixing bowl until pale and fluffy. Add the eggs one at a time, beating well after each addition. Stir in the chocolate mixture until well combined.

3 Sift the flour and cocoa over the mixture and fold in with a metal spoon until evenly mixed. Scrape into the prepared pans, smooth level and bake for 35–40 minutes, or until well risen and firm. Turn out onto wire racks to cool.

COOK'S TIP

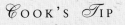

For a richer finish, make a double recipe of buttercream and spread or pipe over the top of the cake as well as using for the filling.

4 Sandwich the cake layers together with the buttercream. Dust with a mixture of confectioners' sugar and cocoa just before serving.

SPECIAL OCCASION CAKES

Any special celebration is a good excuse for indulgence, and nothing could be more indulgent than a luxuriously rich chocolate cake or a lavish Sachertorte. You could try out your skills on a more unusual, impressive Rich Chocolate Leaf Torte, or, alternatively, completely disregard everyone's diet and go totally overboard with one of the richest chocolate cakes ever baked –
Death by Chocolate!

ＳACHERTORTE

Rich and dark, with a wonderful flavor, this glorious confection was created in Vienna in 1832 by Franz Sacher, a chef in the royal household.

INGREDIENTS

8 ounces bittersweet chocolate, broken into squares

⅔ cup unsalted butter, softened

½ cup superfine sugar

8 eggs, separated

1 cup all-purpose flour

For the glaze

1 cup good-quality apricot jam

1 tablespoon lemon juice

For the icing

8 ounces bittersweet chocolate, broken into squares

scant 1 cup superfine sugar

1 tablespoon light corn syrup

1 cup heavy or whipping cream

1 teaspoon vanilla extract

bittersweet chocolate curls, to decorate

~ SERVES 10–12 ~

2 Cream the butter with the sugar in a mixing bowl until pale and fluffy, then add the egg yolks, one at a time, beating after each addition. Beat in the melted chocolate, then sift the flour over the mixture and fold it in evenly.

3 Whisk the egg whites in a clean, grease-free bowl until stiff, then stir about a quarter of the whites into the chocolate mixture to lighten it. Fold in the remaining whites.

4 Pour the mixture into the prepared pan and make level. Bake for about 50-55 minutes, or until firm. Turn out carefully onto a wire rack to cool.

5 Make the glaze. Heat the apricot jam with the lemon juice in a small saucepan until melted, then strain through a sieve into a bowl. Once the cake has cooled, slice in half across the middle to make two even layers.

7 Make the icing. Mix the chocolate, sugar, corn syrup, cream and vanilla extract in a heavy saucepan. Heat gently, stirring constantly, until the mixture is thick and smooth. Simmer gently for 3-4 minutes, without stirring, until the mixture registers 200°F on a candy thermometer. Pour the icing quickly over the cake, spreading to cover the top and side completely. Leave to set, decorate with chocolate curls, then serve with whipped cream if wished.

COOK'S TIP

Use the finest dark chocolate you can afford to make this torte – the expense will be amply justified.

1 Preheat the oven to 350°F. Grease a 9-inch springform cake pan and line it with baking parchment or wax paper. Melt the chocolate in a heat proof bowl over hot water, then remove from the heat.

6 Spread the top and sides of each layer with the apricot glaze, then sandwich them together. Place on a wire rack.

CHOCOLATE ROULADE

WITH COCONUT WHISKEY CREAM

A ravishing roulade topped with curls of fresh coconut, perfect for that special anniversary.

INGREDIENTS

¾ cup superfine sugar

5 eggs, separated

½ cup unsweetened cocoa

For the filling

1¼ cups heavy or whipping cream

3 tablespoons whiskey

2-ounce piece solid creamed coconut

2 tablespoons superfine sugar

For the topping

coarsely grated curls of fresh coconut

chocolate curls

SERVES 8

1 Preheat the oven to 350°F. Grease a 13 x 9-inch jelly roll pan and line it with baking parchment or wax paper. Use 2 tablespoons of the sugar to dust a sheet of wax paper.

2 Place the yolks in a heat proof bowl over hot water. Add the remaining sugar and beat with an electric mixer until the mixture separates into strands when the beaters are lifted. Sift the cocoa over the top and fold in.

3 Whisk the egg whites in a clean, grease-free bowl until they form soft peaks. Fold about 1 tablespoon of the whites into the chocolate mixture to lighten it, then fold in the rest evenly.

4 Pour the mixture into the prepared pan, filling in the corners. Smooth the surface with a spatula, then bake for 20-25 minutes, or until well risen and springy to the touch.

5 Turn the roulade out onto the sugar-dusted wax paper and carefully peel off the lining paper. Cover with a damp, clean dish towel and leave to cool.

6 Make the filling. Beat the cream with the whiskey in a bowl until the mixture just holds its shape, then finely grate the creamed coconut and stir it in, along with the sugar.

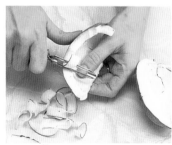

7 Uncover the roulade and spread about three-quarters of the cream mixture out to the edges. Roll up carefully from a long side. Transfer to a plate, pipe or spoon the remaining cream mixture on top, then decorate with the coconut and chocolate curls.

WHITE CHOCOLATE CAPPUCCINO CAKE

INGREDIENTS

4 eggs

½ cup superfine sugar

1 tablespoon strong black coffee

½ teaspoon vanilla extract

1 cup all-purpose flour

3 ounces white chocolate, coarsely grated

For the filling

½ cup heavy or whipping cream

1 tablespoon coffee liqueur

For the frosting and topping

1 tablespoon coffee liqueur

1 recipe White Chocolate Frosting

white chocolate curls

unsweetened cocoa or ground cinnamon, for dusting

SERVES 8

COOK'S TIP

If you don't have any coffee liqueur, use brandy or dark rum instead. For an alcohol-free version, substitute strong black coffee.

> *Luscious, lavish and laced with liqueur, this is strictly for adults only!*

1 Preheat the oven to 350°F. Grease two 8-inch round layer cake pans and line the base of each with a circle of baking parchment or wax paper.

2 Combine the eggs, sugar, coffee and vanilla extract in a large heat proof bowl. Place over a saucepan of hot water and whisk until the mixture is pale and separates into long strands which hold when the whisk is lifted.

3 Sift half the flour over the mixture; fold in gently and evenly. Carefully fold in the remaining flour with the grated white chocolate.

4 Divide the mixture between the prepared pans. Bake for 20-25 minutes, or until the layers are firm and golden brown, then turn out onto wire racks and let cool completely.

5 Make the filling. Whip the cream with the coffee liqueur in a bowl until it forms stiff peaks. Spread over one of the cakes, then place the second layer on top.

6 Stir the coffee liqueur into the frosting. Spread over the top and sides of the cake, swirling with a metal frosting knife. Top the cake with curls of white chocolate and dust with cocoa or cinnamon.

CHOCOLATE RED CURRANT TORTE

> *Red currants are perfect partners for chocolate in this glossy torte, as their sharp-sweet flavor balances the rich chocolate beautifully.*

INGREDIENTS

½ cup unsalted butter, softened

⅔ cup dark brown sugar

2 eggs

⅔ cup sour cream

1¼ cups self-rising flour

1 teaspoon baking powder

3 tablespoons unsweetened cocoa

¾ cup stemmed red currants, plus 1 cup red currant sprigs, to decorate

For the icing

5 ounces bittersweet chocolate, broken into squares

3 tablespoons red currant jelly

2 tablespoons dark rum

½ cup heavy or whipping cream

SERVES 8–10

COOK'S TIP

If red currants are not available, use other small, soft fruits such as raspberries or black currants instead.

1 Preheat the oven to 350°F. ~ Grease a 10-inch tube pan and dust lightly with flour. Cream the butter with the sugar in a mixing bowl until pale and fluffy. Add the eggs and sour cream and beat until the batter is thoroughly combined.

2 Sift the flour, baking ~ powder and cocoa over the mixture, then fold in lightly and evenly. Fold in the stemmed red currants.

3 Spoon the mixture into ~ the prepared pan and smooth the surface. Bake for 40–50 minutes, or until the cake is well risen and firm. Turn out onto a wire rack and let cool completely.

4 Make the icing. Mix the ~ chocolate, red currant jelly and rum in a heat proof bowl. Place the bowl over simmering water and heat gently, stirring occasionally, until melted. Remove from the heat and stir in the cream.

5 Transfer the cooled cake to ~ a serving plate. Spoon the icing evenly over the cake, allowing it to drizzle down the sides. Decorate with red currant sprigs just before serving.

CHOCOLATE ALMOND MOUSSE CAKE

INGREDIENTS

2 ounces bittersweet chocolate, broken into squares

7 ounces marzipan, grated or chopped

⅞ cup milk

1 cup self-rising flour

2 eggs, separated

½ cup light brown sugar

For the mousse filling

4 ounces bittersweet chocolate, broken into squares

4 tablespoons unsalted butter

2 eggs, separated

2 tablespoons almond-flavored liqueur, such as Amaretto di Saronno

For the topping

1 recipe Chocolate Ganache toasted sliced almonds, to decorate

~ SERVES 8 ~

Surrender to the taste sensation of this superb combination of chocolate and almonds.

1 Preheat the oven to 375°F. ~ Grease a deep 8-inch square cake pan and line with baking parchment or wax paper. Combine the chocolate, marzipan and milk in a saucepan and heat gently without boiling, stirring occasionally, until the mixture has melted and is smooth.

2 Sift the flour into a bowl ~ and add the chocolate mixture and egg yolks, beating until evenly mixed.

3 Whisk the egg whites in a ~ clean, grease-free bowl until stiff enough to hold firm peaks. Whisk in the sugar gradually. Stir about 1 tablespoon of the whites into the chocolate mixture to lighten it, then fold in the rest.

4 Spoon the mixture into the ~ pan, spreading it evenly. Bake for 45-50 minutes, until well risen, firm and springy to the touch. Let the cake cool on a wire rack.

5 Make the mousse filling. ~ Melt the chocolate with the butter in a heat proof bowl over barely simmering water, then remove from the heat and beat in the egg yolks and liqueur. Whisk the egg whites in a clean, grease-free bowl until stiff, then fold into the chocolate mixture.

COOK'S TIP

It is important that the chocolate mixture is hot when you beat in the yolks, so that they cook slightly.

6 Slice the cooled cake in ~ half across the middle to make two even layers. Return one half to the clean cake pan and pour over the chocolate mousse. Top with the second layer of cake and press down lightly. Chill until set.

7 Turn the cake out onto a ~ serving plate. Spread the chocolate ganache over the top and sides, then decorate the sides with toasted, sliced almonds. Serve chilled.

DEATH BY CHOCOLATE

INGREDIENTS

8 ounces bittersweet chocolate, broken
into squares

½ cup unsalted butter

⅔ cup milk

1¼ cups light brown sugar

2 teaspoons vanilla extract

2 eggs, separated

⅔ cup sour cream

2 cups self-rising flour

1 teaspoon baking powder

For the filling and topping

4 tablespoons seedless
raspberry jam

4 tablespoons brandy

14 ounces bittersweet chocolate,
broken into squares

⅞ cup unsalted butter

1 recipe Chocolate Ganache

dark and white chocolate curls,
to decorate

~ SERVES 16–20 ~

One of the richest chocolate cakes ever, this should be served in thin slices. True chocoholics can always come back for more!

1 Preheat the oven to 350°F. Grease a deep 9-inch springform cake pan and line the base with baking parchment or wax paper. Place the chocolate, butter and milk in a saucepan. Stir over low heat until smooth. Remove from the heat, beat in the sugar and vanilla, then cool slightly.

2 Beat the egg yolks and cream in a bowl, then beat into the chocolate mixture. Sift the flour and baking powder over the surface and fold in.

3 Whisk the egg whites in a grease-free bowl until stiff; fold into the mixture.

4 Pour into the prepared tin and bake for about 45–55 minutes, or until firm to the touch. Cool in the pan for 15 minutes, then invert onto a wire rack to cool.

5 Slice the cooled cake across the middle to make three even layers. Make the filling. In a small saucepan, warm the jam with 1 tablespoon of the brandy, then brush over two of the layers; let set. Place the remaining brandy in a pan with the chocolate and butter. Heat gently, stirring, until smooth. Cool until the mixture starts to thicken.

6 Spread the bottom layer of the cake with half the chocolate filling, taking care not to disturb the jam. Top with a second layer, jam side up, and spread with the remaining filling. Top with the final layer and press lightly.

7 Let set, then spread the top and sides of the cake with the chocolate ganache. Decorate the cake with chocolate curls and, if desired, chocolate-dipped fresh raspberries.

COOK'S TIP

You may find it easier to reassemble the cake in the clean cake tin. Turn it onto a plate when set, then cover with chocolate ganache.

BLACK FOREST CAKE

This luscious light chocolate sponge, moistened with Kirsch and layered with cherries and cream, is still one of the most popular chocolate cakes.

INGREDIENTS

6 eggs

scant 1 cup superfine sugar

1 teaspoon vanilla extract

½ cup all-purpose flour

½ cup unsweetened cocoa

½ cup unsalted butter, melted

For the filling and topping

4 tablespoons Kirsch

2½ cups double or whipping cream

2 tablespoons confectioners' sugar

½ teaspoon vanilla extract

1½-pound jar pitted morello cherries, drained

To decorate

confectioners' sugar, for dusting

grated chocolate

chocolate curls

fresh or drained canned morello cherries

SERVES 8–10

1 Preheat the oven to 350°F. Grease three 8-inch layer cake pans and line the base of each with a circle of baking parchment or wax paper. Whisk the eggs with the sugar and vanilla extract in a bowl until pale and very thick – the mixture should separate into long strands when the whisk is lifted.

2 Sift the flour and cocoa over the mixture and fold in lightly and evenly. Stir in the melted butter.

3 Divide the mixture evenly among the prepared cake pans, smoothing them level. Bake for 15-18 minutes, until well risen and springy to the touch. Let cool in the pans for about 5 minutes, then turn them out onto wire racks and let cool completely.

4 Prick each layer all over with a skewer or fork, then sprinkle with Kirsch. Whip the cream in a bowl until it starts to thicken, then beat in the confectioners' sugar and vanilla extract until the mixture begins to form soft peaks.

5 Spread one cake layer with a thick layer of whipped cream and top with a quarter of the cherries. Spread a second layer with whipped cream and cherries, then place it on top of the first layer. Top with the final layer.

6 Frost the cake with the remaining whipped cream. Transfer the cake to a plate dusted with confectioners' sugar. Cover the sides with grated chocolate and decorate the cake with the chocolate curls and cherries.

MERINGUE PYRAMID WITH CHOCOLATE MASCARPONE

Roses spell romance for this impressive cake. It makes the perfect centerpiece for a celebration buffet table, and most of the preparation can be done in advance.

INGREDIENTS

4 egg whites

pinch of salt

¾ cup superfine sugar

1 teaspoon ground cinnamon

3 ounces bittersweet chocolate, grated

confectioners' sugar and rose petals, to decorate

For the filling

4 ounces semisweet chocolate

1 teaspoon vanilla extract or rosewater

½ cup mascarpone cheese

SERVES ABOUT 10

1 Preheat the oven to 300°F. Line two large baking sheets with baking parchment or wax paper. Whisk the egg whites with the salt in a clean, grease-free bowl until they form stiff peaks.

2 Gradually whisk in half the sugar, then add the rest and whisk until the meringue is very stiff and glossy. Add the cinnamon and chocolate and whisk lightly to mix.

3 Draw an 8-inch circle on the lining paper on one of the baking sheets, turn it upside-down, and spread the marked circle evenly with about half the meringue. Spoon the remaining meringue in 28-30 teaspoonfuls on both baking sheets. Bake for 1-1½ hours, or until crisp.

4 Make the filling. Melt the chocolate in a heat proof bowl over hot water. Cool slightly, then stir in the vanilla extract and mascarpone. Cool the mixture until firm.

5 Spoon the chocolate mixture into a large piping bag and sandwich the meringues together in pairs, reserving a small amount of filling for the pyramid.

6 Arrange the filled meringues on a serving platter, piling them up in a pyramid and keeping them in position with a few well-placed dabs of the reserved filling. Dust the pyramid with confectioners' sugar, sprinkle with the rose petals and serve.

COOK'S TIP

The meringues can be made up to a week in advance and stored in an airtight container in a cool, dry place.

RICH CHOCOLATE LEAF CAKE

> *Thick, creamy chocolate ganache and chocolate leaves decorate this mouth-watering cake.*

INGREDIENTS

⅔ cup milk

3 ounces bittersweet chocolate, broken into squares

¾ cup unsalted butter, softened

1½ cups light brown sugar

3 eggs

2¼ cups all-purpose flour

2 teaspoons baking powder

5 tablespoons light cream

For the filling and topping

4 tablespoons seedless raspberry preserves

1 recipe Chocolate Ganache

dark and white chocolate leaves

SERVES 12–14

1 Preheat the oven to 375°F. Grease two 9-inch layer cake pans and line the bottom of each with baking parchment or wax paper. Place the milk and chocolate in a saucepan and stir over low heat until the chocolate has melted. Let cool slightly.

2 Cream the butter with the sugar in a mixing bowl until pale and fluffy. Beat in the eggs one at a time, beating well after each addition.

3 Sift the flour and baking powder over the mixture and fold in. Stir in the melted chocolate mixture with the cream, mixing until smooth.

4 Divide evenly between the prepared pans. Bake for 30–35 minutes, or until the cakes are well risen and firm to the touch. Cool in the pans for a few minutes before turning out onto wire racks.

COOK'S TIP

Make a mixture of dark, milk and white chocolate leaves, or marble the mixtures for a variegated effect. Prepare the chocolate leaves in advance to save time, and store them in a covered container in a cool, dry place.

5 Sandwich the cake layers together with the raspberry preserves.

6 Spread the chocolate ganache over the top and sides of the cake, swirling the ganache with a knife. Place the cake on a serving plate, then decorate with the dark and white chocolate leaves.

CARIBBEAN CHOCOLATE RING WITH RUM SYRUP

Lavish and colorful, this exotic chocolate cake can be made in advance, then, just before serving, add the syrup and fruit.

INGREDIENTS

½ cup unsalted butter

¾ cup light brown sugar

2 eggs, beaten

2 ripe bananas, mashed

2 tablespoons shredded coconut

2 tablespoons sour cream

1 cup self-rising flour

½ teaspoon baking soda

3 tablespoons cocoa

For the syrup

½ cup superfine sugar

4 tablespoons water

2 tablespoons dark rum

2 ounces bittersweet chocolate, chopped

To decorate

mixture of tropical fruits, such as mango, papaya, starfruit, and banana

chocolate shapes or curls

SERVES 8–10

1 Preheat the oven to 350°F. Grease a 10-inch tube pan with unsalted butter or vegetable shortening.

2 Cream the butter and sugar until light and fluffy. Beat in the eggs gradually and thoroughly, then mix in the bananas, coconut and cream.

3 Sift the flour, cocoa and baking soda over the mixture and fold in thoroughly and evenly.

4 Pour into the prepared tin and spread evenly. Bake for 45–50 minutes, until firm to the touch. Cool for about 10 minutes in the pan, then turn out to finish cooling on a wire rack.

6 Add the rum and chocolate and stir until melted and smooth, then spread evenly over the cake.

5 For the syrup, place the sugar and water in a pan and heat gently until dissolved. Bring to a boil and boil rapidly for 2 minutes. Remove the pan from the heat.

7 Decorate the cake with tropical fruits and chocolate shapes or curls.

COOK'S TIP

For a really good flavor, use a good-quality bittersweet chocolate for the syrup.

CHOCOLATE BRANDY SNAP GATEAU

INGREDIENTS

9 ounces bittersweet chocolate, broken into squares

1 cup unsalted butter, softened

1 cup firmly packed dark brown sugar

6 eggs, separated

1 teaspoon vanilla extract

1¼ cups ground hazelnuts

4 tablespoons fresh white bread crumbs

finely grated zest of 1 large orange

1 recipe Chocolate Ganache, for filling and frosting

confectioners' sugar, for dusting

For the brandy snaps

4 tablespoons unsalted butter

¼ cup superfine sugar

⅓ cup light corn syrup

½ cup all-purpose flour

1 teaspoon brandy

↞ SERVES 8 ↠

Take your time and savor every mouthful of this sensational dark chocolate cake topped with crisp brandy snaps.

---

1 Preheat the oven to 350°F.
~ Grease two 8-inch layer cake pans and line the base of each with baking parchment or wax paper. Melt the chocolate in a heat proof bowl placed over a pan of hot water. Remove from the heat.

2 Cream the butter with the
~ sugar in a mixing bowl until pale and fluffy. Beat in the egg yolks and vanilla extract. Add the chocolate and mix thoroughly.

3 In a clean, grease-free
~ bowl, whisk the egg whites to soft peaks, then fold them into the chocolate mixture with the ground hazelnuts, bread crumbs and orange zest.

4 Divide the cake mixture
~ evenly between the prepared pans. Bake for 25-30 minutes, or until well risen and firm. Turn out the layers onto wire racks.

5 Make the brandy snaps.
~ Line two baking sheets with baking parchment or wax paper. Heat the butter, sugar and syrup in a saucepan over low heat, stirring occasionally until smooth. Remove from the heat and stir in the flour and brandy.

6 Place small spoonfuls of the
~ batter on the baking sheets and bake for 10-15 minutes, until golden. Cool for a few seconds until firm enough to transfer to a wire rack.

7 Immediately pinch the
~ edges of each cookie to make a frill. If the cookies get too firm, return to the oven for a few minutes. Let set.

8 Sandwich the cake layers
~ together with half the chocolate ganache, transfer to a plate and spread the remaining ganache on top.

9 Arrange the brandy snaps
~ over the cake and dust with confectioners' sugar.

COOK'S TIP

To save time, you could use store-bought brandy snaps — simply warm them for a few minutes in the oven to make them pliable enough for shaping.

STRAWBERRY CHOCOLATE VALENTINE CAKE

INGREDIENTS

1½ cups self-rising flour

2 teaspoons baking powder

5 tablespoons unsweetened cocoa

½ cup superfine sugar

2 eggs, beaten

1 tablespoon molasses

⅔ cup sunflower oil

⅔ cup milk

For the filling

3 tablespoons strawberry jam

⅔ cup heavy or whipping cream

4 ounces strawberries, sliced

To decorate

1 recipe Chocolate Fondant

milk chocolate hearts

confectioners' sugar, for dusting

SERVES 8

> *Offering a slice of this voluptuous Valentine cake could be the start of a very special romance.*

2 Add the eggs, molasses, oil and milk to the well. Mix with a spoon to incorporate the dry ingredients, then beat with a hand-held electric mixer until the mixture is smooth and creamy.

3 Pour the mixture into the prepared cake pan and spread evenly. Bake for about 45 minutes, until well risen and firm to the touch. Cool in the tin for a few minutes, then turn out onto a wire rack to cool completely.

5 Whip the cream in a bowl until it forms stiff peaks. Stir in the strawberries, then spread over the jam. Top with the remaining cake layer.

6 Spread the fondant evenly over the cake. Decorate with chocolate hearts and dust with confectioners' sugar.

1 Preheat the oven to 325°F. Grease a deep 8-inch heart-shaped cake pan and line the base with baking parchment or wax paper. Sift the flour, baking powder and cocoa into a mixing bowl. Stir in the sugar, then make a well in the center.

4 Using a sharp knife, slice the cake neatly into two layers. Place the bottom layer on a plate and spread with strawberry jam.

COOK'S TIP

Keep the fondant tightly covered until you are ready to use it, since the surface dries out fairly quickly. If this happens, the smooth effect will be spoiled.

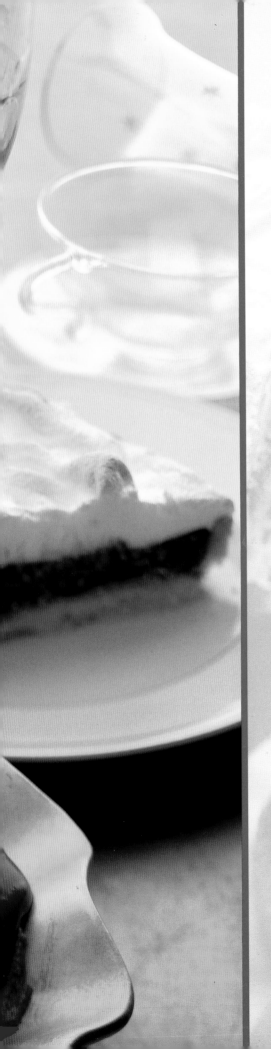

Hot Puddings

Hot chocolate puddings appeal to anyone who craves comforting food – the sweet smell of warm chocolate from a Rich Chocolate Brioche Pudding as it cooks is hard to resist, and just the sight of puddings like Chocolate Chip and Banana Pudding will warm a winter's day. But if you're looking for something a little special for a dinner party, offer slices of crisp, spiced Chocolate, Date and Almond Filo Rolls or luscious poached pears swathed in Chocolate Fudge Blankets.

CHOCOLATE AND ORANGE SCOTCH PANCAKES

Flip for these fabulous baby pancakes in a rich creamy orange liqueur sauce. Serve them straight from the pan to enjoy them at their best.

INGREDIENTS

1 cup self-rising flour

2 tablespoons unsweetened cocoa

2 eggs

2 ounces semisweet chocolate, broken into squares

⅞ cup milk

finely grated zest of 1 orange

2 tablespoons orange juice

butter or oil for frying

4 tablespoons chocolate curls, for sprinkling

For the sauce

2 large oranges

2 tablespoons unsalted butter

3 tablespoons light brown sugar

1 cup crème fraîche

2 tablespoons Grand Marnier or Cointreau

chocolate curls, to decorate

 SERVES 4

1 Sift the flour and cocoa into a bowl and make a well in the center. Add the eggs and beat well, gradually incorporating the surrounding dry ingredients to make a smooth batter.

2 Mix the chocolate and milk in a saucepan. Heat gently until the chocolate has melted, then beat into the batter until smooth and bubbly. Stir the orange zest and juice into the chocolate mixture.

3 Heat a large, heavy frying pan or griddle. Grease with a little butter or oil. Drop 2 tablespoons of batter onto the hot surface, leaving room for spreading. When the pancakes are lightly browned underneath and bubbly on top, flip them over to cook the other side. Slide onto a plate and keep hot, then continue on in the same way.

4 Make the sauce. Grate the zest of 1 orange into a bowl and set aside. Peel both oranges, taking care to remove all the pith, then slice the orange into thin sections.

5 Heat the butter and sugar in a wide, shallow pan over low heat, stirring until the sugar dissolves. Stir in the crème fraîche and heat gently.

6 Add the pancakes and orange slices to the sauce, heat gently for 1-2 minutes, then top with the liqueur. Sprinkle with the reserved orange zest. Sprinkle with the chocolate curls and serve the pancakes at once.

$\mathcal{H}$OT CHOCOLATE ZABAGLIONE

> *Once you've tasted this sensuous dessert,*
> *you'll never look at cocoa in*
> *quite the same way again.*

INGREDIENTS

6 egg yolks

⅔ cup superfine sugar

3 tablespoons unsweetened cocoa

scant 1 cup Marsala

unsweetened cocoa or
confectioners' sugar, for dusting

☞ SERVES 6 ☜

1 Fill a medium saucepan
~ halfway with water and
bring to a simmer. Select a
heat proof bowl which will fit
over the pan, place the the egg
yolks and sugar in it, and
whisk until the mixture is pale
and all the sugar has dissolved.

2 Add the cocoa and Marsala,
~ then place the bowl over
the simmering water. Beat with
a hand-held electric
mixer until the mixture is
smooth, thick and foamy.

3 Pour quickly into tall
~ glasses, dust lightly with
cocoa or confectioners' sugar
and serve immediately, with
Chocolate Cinnamon Tuiles or
amaretti cookies.

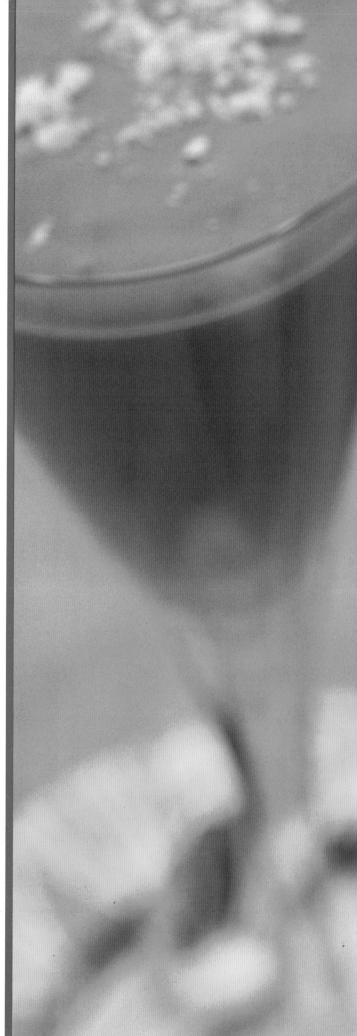

RICH CHOCOLATE BRIOCHE PUDDING

This scrumptious baked dessert may be based on good old bread and butter pudding, but chocolate, brioche and bitter marmalade give it superstar status.

INGREDIENTS

7 ounces semisweet chocolate, broken into squares

4 tablespoons bitter orange marmalade

3 tablespoons unsalted butter

4 individual brioches, or 1 large brioche loaf

3 eggs

1¼ cups milk

1¼ cups cream

2 tablespoons raw sugar

SERVES 4

4 Beat the eggs, milk and cream in a bowl, then pour evenly over the slices. Sprinkle with the raw sugar and bake for 40-50 minutes, until the pudding is lightly set and bubbling. Serve hot.

2 Melt the chocolate with the marmalade and butter in a heat proof bowl over barely simmering water, stirring occasionally.

1 Preheat the oven to 350°F. Lightly butter a shallow casserole.

3 Slice the brioche(s), and spread the melted chocolate mixture over the slices. Arrange them so that they overlap in the dish.

COOK'S TIP

Almost any bread can be used instead of brioche, except savory varieties. Try sliced soft white rolls, buns or French bread for a change.

CHOCOLATE CHIP AND BANANA PUDDING

Hot and steamy, this superb light pudding has a beguiling banana and chocolate flavor.

INGREDIENTS

1¾ cups self-rising flour

6 tablespoons unsalted butter or margarine

2 ripe bananas

⅓ cup super fine sugar

4 tablespoons milk

1 egg, beaten

4 tablespoons semisweet chocolate chips or chopped semisweet chocolate

Glossy Chocolate Sauce, to serve

SERVES 4

1 Fill a saucepan halfway with water and bring it to a boil. Grease a 4-cup heat proof bowl. Sift the flour into a bowl and cut in the unsalted butter or margarine until the mixture resembles coarse breadcrumbs.

2 Peel the bananas and cut them into chunks. Place the pieces of banana in a bowl and mash them until smooth. Stir them into the creamed mixture, with the superfine sugar.

3 Whisk the milk with the egg in a bowl, then beat into the pudding mixture. Stir in the chocolate chips or chopped chocolate.

4 Spoon the mixture into the prepared bowl, cover closely with a double thickness of foil, and steam for 2 hours, adding water to the pan as required during cooking.

5 Run a knife around the top of the pudding to loosen it, then turn it out onto a serving dish. Serve hot, topped with chocolate sauce.

COOK'S TIP

If you have a food processor, make a quick-and-easy version by processing all the ingredients except the chocolate until smooth. Stir in the chocolate and proceed as in the recipe.

MAGIC CHOCOLATE MUD PUDDING

A popular favorite, which magically separates into a light and luscious sponge and a velvety chocolate sauce.

INGREDIENTS

4 tablespoons butter

1 cup light brown sugar, firmly packed

2 cups milk

1 cup self-rising flour

1 teaspoon ground cinnamon

5 tablespoons unsweetened cocoa

strained plain yogurt or vanilla ice cream, to serve

SERVES 4

1 Preheat the oven to 350°F. Lightly grease a 1½ quart casserole and place it on a baking sheet.

2 Place the butter in a saucepan. Add ¾ cup of the sugar and ⅔ cup of the milk. Heat gently, stirring from time to time until the butter has melted and all the sugar has dissolved. Remove the pan from the heat.

3 Sift the flour, cinnamon and 1 tablespoon of the cocoa into the pan and stir into the mixture, mixing evenly. Pour the mixture into the prepared dish and even out the surface.

4 Sift the remaining sugar and cocoa into a bowl, mix well, then sprinkle over the pudding mixture.

5 Pour the remaining milk over the pudding.

6 Bake for 45–50 minutes or until the pudding has risen to the top of the dish and is firm to the touch. Serve hot, with the yogurt or ice cream.

COOK'S TIP

A soufflé dish or similar straight-sided ovenproof dish is ideal, since it supports the pudding as it rises above the sauce.

CHOCOLATE CREPES WITH PLUMS AND PORT

INGREDIENTS

2 ounces semisweet chocolate, broken into squares

scant 1 cup milk

½ cup cream

2 tablespoons unsweetened cocoa

1 cup all-purpose flour

2 eggs

For the filling

1¼ pounds red or golden plums

¼ cup superfine sugar

2 tablespoons water

2 tablespoons port

¾ cup crème fraîche

For the sauce

5 ounces semisweet chocolate

¾ cup heavy or whipping cream

2 tablespoons port

SERVES 6

> *A good dinner party dessert, this dish can be made in advance and always looks impressive.*

1 Place the chocolate in a
~ saucepan with the milk.
Heat gently until the chocolate has melted. Pour into a blender or food processor and add the cream, cocoa, flour and eggs. Blend until smooth and bubbly, then pour the batter into a bowl and chill for 30 minutes.

2 Meanwhile make the
~ filling. Halve and pit the plums. Place them in a saucepan and add the sugar and water. Bring to a boil, then lower the heat, cover, and simmer for about 10 minutes, or until the plums are tender. Stir in the port; simmer for a another 30 seconds. Remove from the heat and keep warm.

COOK'S TIP

Vary the fruit according to what is in season, using a complementary liqueur. Try cherries with cherry brandy, mandarin orange segments with Grand Marnier or poached pears or apples with Calvados. All will taste wonderful with chocolate.

3 Have a sheet of baking
~ parchment ready. Heat a crêpe pan, grease it lightly with a little oil, then pour in just enough batter to cover the base of the pan, swirling to coat evenly. Cook until the crêpe has set, then flip it over to cook the other side. Slide the crêpe out onto the sheet of paper, then cook 9-11 more crêpes in the same way.

4 Make the sauce. Break the
~ chocolate and combine with the cream in a saucepan. Heat gently, stirring until smooth. Add the port and heat gently, stirring, for 1 minute.

5 Divide the plum filling
~ between the crêpes, add a dollop of crème fraîche to each, and roll them up carefully. Serve in individual bowls, with the chocolate sauce spooned over the top.

CHOCOLATE ALMOND MERINGUE PIE

Treat your tastebuds to the contrasting textures and flavors of fluffy meringue on a velvety smooth chocolate filling in a light orange pastry crust.

INGREDIENTS

1½ cups all-purpose flour

⅓ cup rice flour

⅔ cup unsalted butter

finely grated zest of 1 orange

1 egg yolk

slivered almonds and melted bittersweet chocolate, to decorate

For the filling

5 ounces bittersweet chocolate, broken into squares

4 tablespoons unsalted butter, softened

⅓ cup superfine sugar

2 teaspoons cornstarch

4 egg yolks

¾ cup ground almonds

For the meringue

3 egg whites

⅔ cup superfine sugar

☞ SERVES 6 ☜

1 Sift the flour and ground rice into a bowl. Cut in the butter until the mixture resembles breadcrumbs. Stir in the orange zest. Add the egg yolk; lightly knead the dough. Roll out and use to line a 9-inch tart pan. Chill for 30 minutes.

2 Preheat the oven to 375°F. Prick the pastry shell all over with a fork, cover with wax paper weighed down with dried beans and bake for 10 minutes. Remove the pastry shell from the oven, and take out the dried beans and paper.

3 Make the filling. Melt the chocolate in a heat proof bowl over hot water. Cream the butter with the sugar in a bowl, then beat in the cornstarch and egg yolks. Fold in the almonds, then the chocolate. Spread in the pastry shell. Bake for another 10 minutes.

4 Make the meringue. Whisk the egg whites in a clean, grease-free bowl until stiff, then gradually whisk in about half the superfine sugar. Fold in the remaining sugar.

5 Spoon the meringue over the chocolate filling, lifting it up with the back of the spoon to form peaks. Reduce the oven temperature to 350°F and bake the pie for about 20 minutes or until the topping is pale gold. Serve warm, sprinkled with almonds and drizzled with melted chocolate.

COOK'S TIP

The pastry can be made in a food processor. Pulse all the ingredients in the processor for a few seconds until the pastry just holds together. If too dry, add 1–2 teaspoons water.

CHOCOLATE, DATE AND ALMOND FILO ROLLS

INGREDIENTS

10-ounce package filo pastry, thawed

4 tablespoons unsalted butter, melted

confectioners' sugar, unsweetened cocoa and ground cinnamon, for dusting

For the filling

6 tablespoons unsalted butter

4 ounces bittersweet chocolate, broken into squares

1 cup ground almonds

⅔ cup chopped dates

⅔ cup confectioners' sugar

2 teaspoons rosewater

½ teaspoon ground cinnamon

SERVES 6

Experience the allure of the Middle East with this delectable dessert. Crisp filo pastry conceals a chocolate and rosewater filling studded with dates and almonds.

1 Preheat the oven to 350°F.
~ Grease a 8½ inch layer cake pan. Make the filling. Melt the butter with the chocolate in a heat proof bowl over barely simmering water, then remove from the heat and stir in the remaining ingredients to make a thick paste. Let cool.

2 Lay 1 sheet of filo on a
~ clean work surface (see Cook's Tip). Brush it with melted butter, then lay a second sheet on top and brush with butter.

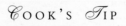

3 Shape a handful of the
~ chocolate almond mixture into a rough log shape and place along one long edge of the layered filo. Roll the pastry tightly around the filling to make a roll.

4 Place the roll around the
~ outside of the tin. Make enough rolls to fill the tin.

5 Brush the rolls with the
~ remaining melted butter. Bake for 30-35 minutes until the pastry is golden brown and crisp. Remove the rolls from the tin; place them on a plate. Serve warm, dusted with confectioners' sugar, cocoa and cinnamon.

COOK'S TIP

Filo pastry dries out very quickly, so remove one sheet at a time and keep the rest covered with a slightly damp, clean dish towel.

PEARS IN CHOCOLATE FUDGE BLANKETS

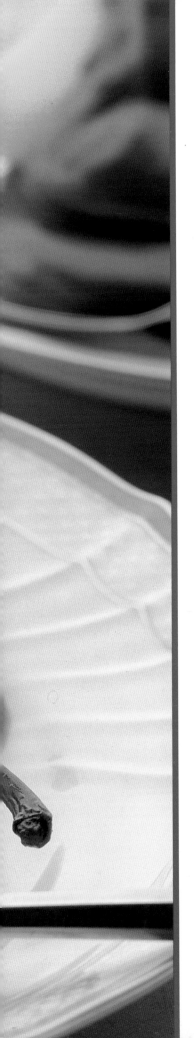

INGREDIENTS

6 ripe pears

2 tablespoons freshly squeezed
lemon juice

⅓ cup superfine sugar

1¼ cups water

1 cinnamon stick

For the sauce

⅞ cup heavy or whipping cream

1 cup light brown sugar

2 tablespoons unsalted butter

4 tablespoons light corn syrup

½ cup milk

7 ounces bittersweet dark chocolate,
broken into squares

⤳ SERVES 6 ⤳

Warm poached pears swathed in a rich chocolate fudge sauce – who could resist such a sensual pleasure?

3 Bring to a boil, then lower
~ the heat, cover the pan and
simmer the pears gently for
15–20 minutes, or until they
are just tender.

4 Meanwhile make the
~ sauce. Place the cream,
sugar, butter, corn syrup and
milk in a heavy saucepan. Heat
gently until the sugar has
dissolved and the butter and
syrup have melted, then bring
to a boil. Boil, stirring
constantly, for about
5 minutes or until the sauce
is thick and smooth. Remove
from the heat and stir in the
chocolate, a few squares at a
time, until melted.

5 Using a slotted spoon,
~ transfer the poached pears
to a dish. Keep hot. Boil the
syrup rapidly to reduce to
about 3–4 tablespoons.
Remove the cinnamon stick
and stir the syrup into the
chocolate sauce.

6 Serve the pears in
~ individual bowls, topped
with the hot chocolate sauce.

1 Peel and core the pears,
~ leaving the stems intact.
Brush the surfaces with freshly
squeezed lemon juice to
prevent browning.

2 Place the sugar and water
~ in a large saucepan. Heat
gently until the sugar dissolves.
Add the pears and cinnamon
stick, along with any
remaining lemon juice and, if
necessary, water, so that the
pears are almost covered.

99

PEACHY CHOCOLATE PUDDING

> *Resist everything except temptation, Oscar Wilde urged. So next time you crave something hot and chocolaty, raid the pantry and whip up this delicious pudding.*

INGREDIENTS

7 ounces bittersweet chocolate, broken into squares

½ cup unsalted butter

4 eggs, separated

½ cup superfine sugar

15 ounces can peach slices, drained

SERVES 6

1 Preheat the oven to 325°F. Butter a wide casserole. Melt the chocolate with the butter in a heat proof bowl over barely simmering water. Remove from the heat.

2 In a bowl, whisk the egg yolks with the sugar until thick and pale. In a clean, grease-free bowl, whisk the whites until stiff.

3 Beat the chocolate into the egg yolk mixture.

4 Fold in the whites lightly and evenly.

5 Fold the peach slices into the mixture, then pour into the prepared dish.

6 Bake for 35–40 minutes, or until risen and just firm. Serve hot, with cream or yogurt if desired.

COOK'S TIP

Don't even out the mixture in the dish before baking, as it looks more interesting if the surface is rough.

PRUNE BEIGNETS IN CHOCOLATE ARMAGNAC SAUCE

¾ cup all-purpose flour

3 tablespoons ground almonds

3 tablespoons oil or melted butter

1 egg white

4 tablespoons water

oil for deep frying

¾ cup prunes

3 tablespoons vanilla sugar

1 tablespoon unsweetened cocoa

For the sauce

7 ounces milk chocolate, broken into squares

½ cup crème fraîche

2 tablespoons Armagnac or brandy

SERVES 4

COOK'S TIP

Vanilla sugar is very popular in parts of Europe, where it is sold in packets. To make your own, add a vanilla bean to a jar of superfine sugar. The sugar will soon take on a subtle vanilla flavor.

> *Go on, indulge yourself! Slide your spoon into silky chocolate sauce, scoop up a feather-light prune beignet and get ready for rapture.*

1 Start by making the sauce. Melt the chocolate in a heat proof bowl over hot water. Remove from the heat, stir in the crème fraîche until smooth, then add the Armagnac or brandy. Replace the bowl over the water (off the heat) so that it stays warm.

2 Beat the flour, almonds, oil or butter and egg white in a bowl, then beat in enough of the water to make a smooth, thick batter.

3 Heat the oil for deep frying to 350°F or until a cube of dried bread browns in 30-45 seconds. Dip the prunes into the batter and fry, a few at a time. The prunes are done when the beignets rise to the surface of the oil and are golden brown and crisp.

4 Remove each successive batch of beignets with a slotted spoon, drain on paper towels and keep hot. Mix the vanilla sugar and cocoa in a bowl or brown paper bag, add the drained beignets and toss well to coat.

5 Serve in individual bowls, with the sauce poured over the top of each serving.

HOT MOCHA RUM SOUFFLES

These superb soufflés always rise to the occasion. Serve them as soon as they are cooked for a fantastic finale to a dinner party.

INGREDIENTS

2 tablespoons unsalted butter, melted

½ cup unsweetened cocoa

⅓ cup superfine sugar

4 tablespoons strong black coffee

2 tablespoons dark rum

6 egg whites

confectioners' sugar, for dusting

SERVES 6

1 Preheat the oven with a baking sheet inside to 375°F. Grease six 1 cup ovenproof ramekins with melted butter.

2 Mix 1 tablespoon of the cocoa with 1 tablespoon of the superfine sugar in a bowl. Pour the mixture into each of the dishes, rotating them so that they are evenly coated.

3 Mix the remaining cocoa with the coffee and rum.

4 Whisk the egg whites in a clean, grease-free bowl until they form stiff peaks. Whisk in the remaining sugar. Stir a generous spoonful of the whites into the cocoa mixture to lighten it, then fold in the remaining whites.

5 Spoon the mixture evenly into the prepared dishes. Place on the hot baking sheet, and bake for 12–15 minutes or until well risen. Serve immediately, dusted with confectioners' sugar.

COOK'S TIP

When serving the soufflés at the end of a dinner party, prepare them just before the meal is served. Put them in the oven as soon as the main course is finished and serve them steaming hot.

Steamed Chocolate and Fruit Puddings with Chocolate Syrup

INGREDIENTS

⅔ cup dark brown sugar

1 Granny Smith apple

¾ cup cranberries,
thawed if frozen

½ cup softened margarine

2 eggs

¾ cup all-purpose flour

½ teaspoon baking powder

3 tablespoons unsweetened cocoa

For the chocolate syrup

4 ounces bittersweet chocolate,
broken into squares

2 tablespoons honey

1 tablespoon unsalted butter

½ teaspoon vanilla extract

SERVES 4

Some things always turn out well, including these wonderful little puddings. Dark, fluffy chocolate sponge cake is topped with tangy cranberries and apple, and served with a honeyed chocolate syrup.

1 Fill a saucepan halfway with water and bring it to a boil. Grease four individual ramekins and sprinkle each one with a thin covering of the brown sugar.

2 Peel and core the apple. Dice it into a bowl, add the cranberries and stir to mix well. Divide the fruit mixture among the prepared ramekins.

3 Place the remaining brown sugar in a mixing bowl. Add the margarine, eggs, flour, baking powder and cocoa; beat the ingredients until combined and smooth.

4 Spoon the mixture into the ramekins. Cover each with a double thickness of foil. Steam for 45 minutes, filling the pan with boiling water as required, until the puddings are well risen and firm.

5 Make the syrup. Mix the chocolate, honey, butter and vanilla extract in a small saucepan. Heat gently, stirring, until melted and smooth.

6 Run a knife around the edge of each pudding to loosen it, then turn out onto individual plates. Serve at once, with the chocolate syrup.

Cook's Tip

The puddings can be cooked very quickly in the microwave. Use non-metallic dishes and cover with wax paper instead of foil. Cook on High (100% power) for 5–6 minutes, then let stand for 2–3 minutes before turning out.

COLD DESSERTS

Cold desserts mean easy entertaining, since they can be prepared almost entirely in advance. A rich, dark Chocolate Sorbet with Red Berries can be made days before serving, ready to dish up with fresh red fruits, and a Black and White Chocolate Mousse will keep in the fridge for the next day. But don't stop at mousses and ices – if your sweet tooth craves a really lavish treat, how about Raspberry, Mascarpone and White Chocolate Cheesecake, or, for more formal meals, an elegant Chocolate Hazelnut Galette?

BLACK AND WHITE CHOCOLATE MOUSSE

INGREDIENTS

For the white mousse

7 ounces white chocolate,
broken into squares

4 tablespoons white rum

2 tablespoons coconut cream

1 egg yolk

4 tablespoons superfine sugar

1 cup heavy or whipping cream

2 egg whites

For the dark mousse

7 ounces semisweet chocolate,
broken into squares

2 tablespoons unsalted butter

4 tablespoons dark rum

3 eggs, separated

chocolate curls, to decorate

SERVES 8

Dark and dreamy or white and creamy — if you can't decide which mousse you prefer, have both!

1 Make the white chocolate
~ mousse. Melt the chocolate
with the white rum and
coconut cream in a heat proof
bowl over barely simmering
water. Remove from the heat.

2 Beat the egg yolk and sugar
~ in a separate bowl, then
whisk into the chocolate
mixture. Whip the cream until
it begins to form stiff peaks,
then carefully fold it into the
chocolate mixture.

3 Whisk the egg whites in a
~ clean, grease-free bowl
until they form soft peaks,
then fold quickly and evenly
into the chocolate mixture.
Chill until set.

4 Make the dark chocolate
~ mousse. Melt the chocolate
with the butter and dark rum
in a heat proof bowl over
barely simmering water.
Remove from the heat and
beat in the egg yolks.

5 Whisk the egg whites until
~ they form soft peaks, then
fold them quickly and evenly
into the chocolate mixture.
Chill until set.

6 Spoon the white and dark
~ chocolate mixtures
alternately into tall glasses or
into one large glass serving
bowl. Decorate with chocolate
curls and serve.

COOK'S TIP

*Either the white or the
dark chocolate mousse
can be served alone;
simply spoon into small
pots or ramekins and
allow to set.
Alternatively, marble
the mousses.*

CHOCOLATE SORBET WITH RED BERRIES

The chill that thrills — that's chocolate sorbet. For a really fine texture, it helps to have an ice-cream maker, which churns the mixture as it freezes, but you can make it by hand quite easily.

INGREDIENTS

2 cups water

3 tablespoons honey

½ cup superfine sugar

¾ cup unsweetened cocoa

2 ounces bittersweet chocolate,
broken into squares

14 ounces mixed berries such as
raspberries, red currants or strawberries

SERVES 6

2 Remove from the heat,
~ add the chocolate and stir
until melted. Let cool.

3 Pour into an ice-cream
~ maker and churn until
frozen. Alternatively, pour into
a container suitable for use in
the freezer, freeze until slushy,
whisk until smooth, then
freeze again. Whisk for a
second time before the mixture
hardens completely.

4 Remove from the freezer
~ 10-15 minutes before
serving, to soften the sorbet.
Serve scooped into ice-cream
bowls, topped with the berries.

1 Place the water, honey,
~ sugar and cocoa in a
saucepan. Heat gently, stirring
occasionally, until the sugar has
completely dissolved.

COOK'S TIP

*This sorbet looks
attractive if served in
small oval scoops shaped
with two spoons — simply
scoop out the sorbet with
one tablespoon, then use
another to smooth it off
and transfer it to
a bowl.*

RASPBERRY, MASCARPONE AND WHITE CHOCOLATE CHEESECAKE

INGREDIENTS

4 tablespoons unsalted butter

8 ounces gingersnap cookies, crushed

½ cup chopped pecans
or walnuts

For the filling

1¼ cups mascarpone cheese

¾ cup ricotta cheese

2 eggs, beaten

3 tablespoons superfine sugar

9 ounces white chocolate,
broken into squares

1½ cups fresh or
frozen raspberries

For the topping

½ cup mascarpone cheese

⅓ cup ricotta cheese

white chocolate curls and raspberries,
to decorate

SERVES 8

Raspberries and white chocolate are an irresistible combination, especially when teamed with rich mascarpone on a crunchy ginger and pecan base.

1 Preheat the oven to 300°F.
~ Melt the butter in a
saucepan, then stir in the
crushed gingersnaps and nuts.
Press into the bottom of a
9-inch springform pan.

2 Make the filling. Beat the
~ mascarpone and ricotta in
a bowl, then beat in the eggs
and superfine sugar until
evenly mixed.

3 Melt the white chocolate
~ gently in a heat proof bowl
over hot water, then stir into
the cheese mixture with the
fresh or frozen raspberries.

4 Pour into the prepared pan
~ and spread evenly, then
bake for about 1 hour or until
just set. Switch off the oven,
but do not remove the
cheesecake. Leave it in until
cooled and completely set.

5 Remove the sides of the
~ pan and carefully lift the
cheesecake onto a serving
plate. Make the topping by
mixing the mascarpone and
ricotta in a bowl and spreading
the mixture over the
cheesecake. Decorate with
chocolate curls and raspberries.

COOK'S TIP

The cookies for the crust should be crushed quite finely. This can be easily done in a food processor. Alternatively, place the cookies in a sturdy plastic bag and crush them with a rolling pin.

DEVILISH CHOCOLATE ROULADE

INGREDIENTS

6 ounces bittersweet dark chocolate, broken into squares

4 eggs, separated

½ cup superfine sugar

chocolate-dipped strawberries, to decorate

unsweetened cocoa for dusting

For the filling

8 ounces semisweet chocolate, broken into squares

3 tablespoons brandy

2 eggs, separated

1 cup mascarpone cheese

SERVES 6–8

> *A decadent dessert for a party or a dinner à deux: the cake can be made a day or two ahead, then filled and rolled on the day of serving.*

1 Preheat the oven to 350°F. Grease a 13 x 9 inch jelly roll pan and line with baking parchment or wax paper. Melt the chocolate in a heat proof bowl.

2 Whisk the egg yolks and sugar in a bowl until pale and thick, then stir in the melted chocolate evenly.

3 In a clean, grease-free bowl, whisk the egg whites to soft peaks, then fold lightly and evenly into the egg and chocolate mixture.

4 Pour mixture into the pan and spread to the corners. Bake for 15-20 minutes, until well risen and firm to the touch. Dust a sheet of wax paper with cocoa. Turn the cake out on the paper, cover with a clean dish towel and leave to cool.

COOK'S TIP

Don't worry if the roulade cracks – it's meant to!

5 Make the filling. Melt the chocolate with the brandy in a heat proof bowl over hot water. Remove from the heat. Beat the egg yolks together, then beat into the chocolate mixture. In a separate bowl, whisk the whites to soft peaks, then fold them lightly and evenly into the filling.

6 Uncover the cake, remove the wax paper and spread with the mascarpone. Spread the chocolate mixture over the top, then carefully roll up the cake from a long side to enclose the filling. Transfer to a serving plate, top with chocolate-dipped strawberries and dust with unsweetened cocoa.

Tiramisu in Chocolate Cups

INGREDIENTS

1 egg yolk

2 tablespoons superfine sugar

½ teaspoon vanilla extract

1 cup mascarpone cheese

½ cup strong black coffee

1 tablespoon unsweetened cocoa

2 tablespoons coffee liqueur

16 amaretti cookies

bittersweet cocoa,
for dusting

For the chocolate cups

6 ounces bittersweet chocolate,
broken into squares

2 tablespoons unsalted butter

⁓ SERVES 6 ⁓

1 Make the chocolate cups.
⁓ Cut out six 6-inch circles
of baking parchment or wax
paper. Melt the chocolate with
the butter in a heat proof bowl
over barely simmering water.
Stir until smooth, then spread
a spoonful of the chocolate
mixture over each circle, to
within ¾ inch of the edge.

> *Give in to the temptation of tiramisù,
> with its magical mocha flavor.*

2 Carefully lift each paper
⁓ circle and drape it over an
upturned teacup or ramekin so
that the edges curve into frills.
Chill until completely set, then
carefully lift off and peel away
the paper to reveal the
chocolate cups.

3 Make the filling. Beat the
⁓ egg yolk and sugar in a
bowl until smooth, then stir
in the vanilla extract and
mascarpone. Mix to a smooth
creamy consistency.

4 In a separate bowl, mix the
⁓ coffee, cocoa and liqueur.
Break up the cookies roughly,
then stir into the mixture.

5 Place the chocolate cups
⁓ on individual plates. Divide
half the cookie mixture among
them, then spoon over half the
mascarpone mixture.

6 Spoon over the remaining
⁓ cookie mixture (including
any extra liquid), top with the
rest of the mascarpone mixture
and dust with cocoa. Serve as
soon as possible.

Cook's Tip

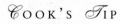

*When spreading the
chocolate for the cups,
don't aim for perfectly
regular edges; uneven
edges will give a more
frilled effect.*

CHOCOLATE ORANGE MARQUISE

There are people who really like chocolate, others who enjoy it now and then, and some who are utterly passionate about the stuff. If you fall into the final category, you'll adore this dense, delectable dessert.

INGREDIENTS

1 cup superfine sugar

4 tablespoons freshly squeezed orange juice

12 ounces bittersweet chocolate, broken into squares

1 cup unsalted butter, cut into pieces

5 eggs

finely grated zest of 1 orange

3 tablespoons all-purpose flour

confectioners' sugar and finely pared strips of orange rind, to decorate

SERVES 6–8

1 Preheat the oven to 350°F. Grease a 9-inch layer cake pan with a depth of 2½ inches. Line the bottom of the pan with a sheet of parchment or wax paper.

2 Place ½ cup of the sugar in a saucepan. Add the orange juice and stir continuously over a low heat until the sugar has dissolved.

3 Remove from the heat and stir in the chocolate until melted, then add the butter, piece by piece, until melted and evenly mixed.

COOK'S TIP

The safest way to add the water to the roasting pan is to place the pan on a rack in the oven, pull the rack out slightly, then pour in boiling water from a teapot. If you pour the water in before transferring the pan to the oven, you will risk spilling it and scalding yourself.

4 Whisk the eggs with the remaining sugar in a large bowl until the mixture is pale and very thick. Add the orange zest. Then, fold the chocolate mixture lightly and evenly into the egg mixture. Sift the flour over the top and fold in evenly.

5 Scrape the mixture into the prepared pan. Place in a roasting pan, transfer to the oven, then pour hot water into the roasting pan to reach about halfway up the sides of the cake pan.

6 Bake for about 1 hour or until the cake is firm to the touch. Remove the cake pan from the bain-marie and cool for 15-20 minutes. Invert the cake on a baking sheet, place a serving plate upside-down on top, then turn plate and baking sheet over together so that the cake is transferred to the plate.

7 Dust with confectioners' sugar, decorate with strips of orange rind and serve slightly warm or chilled.

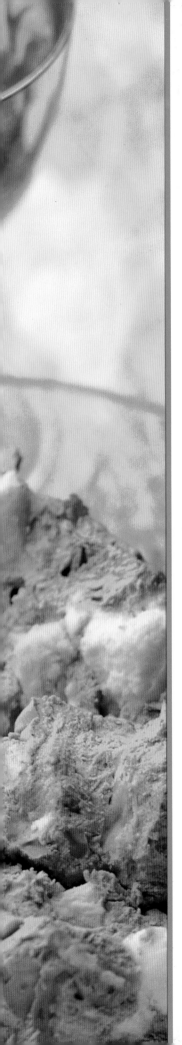

ROCKY ROAD ICE CREAM

For a frozen fudgy treat, there's nothing to beat this classic ice cream packed with contrasting textures and flavors.

INGREDIENTS

4 ounces semisweet chocolate, broken into squares

⅔ cup milk

1¼ cups heavy or whipping cream

1½ cups miniature marshmallows

½ cup candied cherries, chopped

½ cup crumbled shortbread cookies

2 tablespoons chopped walnuts

SERVES 6

2 Whip the cream in a bowl until it forms soft peaks. Beat in the chocolate mixture.

4 Stir the marshmallows, cherries, crushed cookies and nuts into the iced mixture, then return to the freezer container and freeze until firm.

5 Allow the ice cream to soften at room temperature for 15-20 minutes before serving in scoops.

1 Melt the chocolate in the milk in a saucepan over low heat, stirring from time to time. Let the mixture cool completely.

3 Tip the mixture into an ice-cream maker and churn until thick and almost frozen. Alternatively, pour into a container suitable for use in the freezer, freeze until ice crystals form around the edges, then whisk until smooth.

COOK'S TIP

For a quick version, simply stir the flavorings into store-bought soft-serve chocolate ice cream and freeze until firm.

CHOCOLATE CONES WITH APRICOT SAUCE

9 ounces bittersweet chocolate, broken into squares

1½ cups ricotta cheese

3 tablespoons heavy or whipping cream

2 tablespoons brandy

2 tablespoons confectioners' sugar

finely grated zest of 1 lemon

strips of lemon rind, to decorate

For the sauce

⅔ cup apricot jam

3 tablespoons lemon juice

SERVES 6

The seductive liaison of dark chocolate wrapped around a creamy brandy-flavored filling makes a dramatic and delicious dessert. The cones can be made, filled and arranged with the sauce on plates before you start your meal, then chilled, ready to serve.

1 Cut 4-inch double thickness circles from baking parchment or wax paper and shape each into a cone. Secure with masking tape.

2 Melt the chocolate in a heat proof bowl over hot water, cool slightly, then spoon a little into each cone, swirling and brushing it to coat the paper in an even layer.

3 Stand each cone point downward in a cup or glass, to hold it straight. Leave in a cool place until the cones are completely set.

4 Make the sauce. Combine the apricot jam and lemon juice in a small saucepan. Melt over low heat, then cool.

5 Beat the ricotta, cream, brandy and sugar in a bowl. Stir in the lemon zest.

6 Spoon or pipe the ricotta mixture into the cones, then carefully peel off the baking paper.

7 Serve the cones in pairs on individual plates, decorated with lemon rind and surrounded with the cooled apricot sauce.

COOK'S TIP

When making the paper cones, make sure there is no gap at the pointed end, or the chocolate will run out when you coat them. It is best to let the chocolate cool slightly before use, so that it sets quickly.

WHITE CHOCOLATE VANILLA MOUSSE WITH DARK CHOCOLATE SAUCE

INGREDIENTS

7 ounces white chocolate, broken into squares

2 eggs, separated

4 tablespoons superfine sugar

1¼ cups heavy or whipping cream

1 packet powdered gelatin

⅔ cup plain strained yogurt

2 teaspoon vanilla extract

For the sauce

2 ounces semisweet chocolate, broken into squares

2 tablespoons dark rum

4 tablespoons cream

☞ SERVES 6–8 ☜

COOK'S TIP

It is very important to make sure that the gelatin is completely dissolved in the cream before adding it to the other ingredients. Lift a little of the mixture on a wooden spoon to check that no undissolved granules remain. Alternatively, dissolve the gelatin in 2 tablespoons cold water in a cup, then place it over hot water before stirring it into the hot cream.

Happy endings are assured when slices of creamy white chocolate mousse are served with a divine dark sauce.

1 Line a loaf pan with baking parchment or wax paper. Melt the chocolate in a heat proof bowl over a pan of hot water, then remove it from the heat.

2 Whisk the egg yolks and sugar in a bowl until pale and thick, then beat in the melted chocolate.

3 Heat the cream in a small saucepan until almost boiling, then remove from the heat. Sprinkle the powdered gelatin over, stirring until completely dissolved.

4 Then pour onto the chocolate mixture, whisking vigorously to mix until smooth.

5 Whisk the yogurt and vanilla extract into the mixture. In a clean, grease-free bowl, whisk the egg whites until stiff, then fold them into the mixture. Pour evenly into the prepared loaf pan and chill until set.

6 Make the sauce. Melt the chocolate with the rum and cream in a heat proof bowl over barely simmering water, stirring occasionally, then leave to cool completely.

7 When the mousse is set, remove it from the pan with the help of the paper. Serve in thick slices in a pool of cooled chocolate sauce.

ITALIAN CHOCOLATE RICOTTA PIE

2 cups all-purpose flour

2 tablespoons unsweetened cocoa

4 tablespoons superfine sugar

½ cup unsalted butter

4 tablespoons dry sherry

For the filling

2 egg yolks

½ cup confectioners' sugar

2½ cups ricotta cheese

finely grated zest of 1 lemon

6 tablespoons semisweet chocolate chips

5 tablespoons chopped candied lemon peel

3 tablespoons chopped angelica

~ SERVES 6 ~

> *This glorious pie travels well and is perfect for picnics.*

3 Make the filling. Beat the
~ egg yolks and sugar in a bowl, then beat in the ricotta. Mix thoroughly. Stir in the lemon zest, chocolate, candied lemon peel and angelica.

4 Scrape the ricotta mixture
~ into the pastry shell and even out the surface. Roll out the remaining pastry and cut into strips, then arrange these in a lattice over the pie.

5 Bake for 15 minutes, then
~ lower the oven temperature to 350°F and cook for another 30–35 minutes, until the pie is golden brown and firm. Cool in the pan.

COOK'S TIP

This pie is best served at room temperature, so if you make it in advance, refrigerate it and then bring to room temperature for about 30 minutes before serving.

1 Preheat the oven to 400°F.
~ Sift the flour and cocoa into a bowl, then stir in the sugar. Cut in the butter until the mixture resembles bread crumbs, then work in the sherry, using your fingertips, until the mixture binds to a firm dough.

2 Roll out three-quarters of
~ the pastry on a lightly floured surface and line a 9½-inch loose-based tart pan.

CHOCOLATE MANDARIN TRIFLE

INGREDIENTS

4 ladyfingers

14 amaretti cookies

4 tablespoons Amaretto di Saronno or sweet sherry

8 mandarin oranges

For the custard

7 ounces semisweet chocolate, broken into squares

2 tablespoons cornstarch

2 tablespoons confectioners' sugar

2 egg yolks

scant 1 cup milk

1 cup mascarpone cheese

For the topping

1 cup ricotta cheese

chocolate shapes

mandarin orange slices

~ SERVES 6–8 ~

Trifle is always a tempting treat, but when a rich chocolate and mascarpone custard is combined with amaretto and mandarin oranges, it becomes sheer delight.

2 Juice the 2 mandarins and sprinkle into the dish. Separate the rest into segments and put them in the dish.

4 Heat the milk in a small saucepan until almost boiling, then pour onto the egg yolk mixture, stirring constantly. Return to the clean pan and stir over low heat until the custard has thickened slightly and is smooth.

5 Stir in the mascarpone until melted. Add the melted chocolate, mixing it evenly. Spread over the ladyfingers, cool, then chill.

1 Break up the ladyfingers and place them in a large glass serving dish. Crumble the amaretti cookies over them and then sprinkle with amaretto or sweet sherry.

3 Make the custard. Melt the chocolate in a heat proof bowl over hot water. In a separate bowl, mix the cornstarch, sugar and egg yolks to a paste.

6 To finish, spread the ricotta cheese over the custard, then decorate with chocolate shapes and mandarin slices just before serving.

CHOCOLATE AND CHESTNUT POTS

9 ounces semisweet chocolate

4 tablespoons Madeira

2 tablespoons butter, diced

2 eggs, separated

1 cup unsweetened chestnut paste

crème fraîche or whipped cream, to decorate

SERVES 6

These rich little pots, prepared in advance, are the perfect ending for a dinner party. For the very best flavor, remove them from the fridge about 30 minutes before serving to allow them to "ripen."

1 Make a few chocolate curls for decoration, then break the rest of the chocolate into squares and melt it with the Madeira in a saucepan over low heat. Remove from the heat and add the butter, a few pieces at a time, stirring until melted and smooth.

COOK'S TIP

If Madeira is not available, use brandy or rum instead. These chocolate pots can be frozen successfully for up to 2 months.

2 Beat the egg yolks quickly into the mixture, then beat in the chestnut paste, mixing until smooth.

3 Whisk the egg whites in a clean, grease-free bowl until stiff. Stir about 1 tablespoon of the whites into the chestnut mixture to lighten it, then fold in the rest evenly.

4 Spoon the mixture into 6 small ramekins and chill until set. Serve the pots topped with a generous spoonful of crème fraîche or whipped cream. Decorate with the chocolate curls.

CHOCOLATE, BANANA AND TOFFEE PIE

Chocoholics love finding new ways of using their favorite ingredient. Here's how it can help to make a "Banoffee Pie" even more delicious.

INGREDIENTS

5 tablespoons unsalted butter

9 ounces chocolate wafer cookies

chocolate curls to decorate

For the filling

1 can (13 ounces) sweetened condensed milk

5 ounces semisweet chocolate, broken into squares

½ cup crème fraîche or cream

1 tablespoon light corn syrup

For the topping

2 bananas

1 cup crème fraîche

2 tablespoons strong black coffee

SERVES 6

1 Melt the unsalted butter in a saucepan. Crush the chocolate wafers quite finely in a food processor or with a rolling pin. Place the crushed wafers in a bowl and stir in the melted butter. Press onto the base and side of a 9-inch loose-based tart pan. Let set.

2 Make the filling. Place the unopened can of condensed milk in a saucepan of boiling water and cover with a lid. Lower the heat and simmer for 2 hours, replenishing water as necessary. Do not allow to boil dry.

3 Remove the pan from the heat and set aside, covered, until the can has cooled down completely in the water. Do not attempt to open the can until it is completely cooled, as the contents will be under pressure due to the heat.

4 Melt the chocolate with the crème fraîche or cream and light corn syrup in a heat proof bowl over a pan of barely simmering water. Stir in the caramelized condensed milk and beat until evenly mixed, then spread the filling over the cookie crust.

5 Slice the bananas and arrange them over the chocolate filling.

6 Stir together the crème fraîche and coffee, then spoon over the bananas. Decorate liberally with the chocolate curls.

GREEK CHOCOLATE MOUSSE TARTLETS

INGREDIENTS

1 recipe Chocolate Shortcrust Pastry

melted dark chocolate, to decorate

For the filling

7 ounces white chocolate,
broken into squares

½ cup milk

2 teaspoons powdered gelatin

2 tablespoons superfine sugar

1 teaspoon vanilla extract

2 eggs, separated

1 cup plain
strained yogurt

~ SERVES 6 ~

> *Don't be fooled by the filling – it may be yogurt-based, but is just as sinful as all the other sweet sensations in this collection!*

1 Preheat the oven to 375°F. Roll out the pastry and use it to line six small, loose-based tarlet pans.

2 Prick the base of each pastry shell all over with a fork, cover with wax paper weighed down with dried beans and bake for 10 minutes. Remove the dried beans and paper, return to the oven and bake another 15 minutes, or until the pastry is firm. Let the pastry shells cool completely in the pans.

3 Make the filling. Melt the chocolate in a heat proof bowl over hot water. Pour the milk into a saucepan, sprinkle over the powdered gelatin and heat gently, stirring, until the gelatin has dissolved completely. Remove from the heat and stir in the chocolate.

COOK'S TIP

If you prefer, make a large tart instead of individual ones – use a 9-inch tart pan.

4 Whisk the sugar, vanilla extract and egg yolks in a large bowl, then beat in the chocolate mixture. Beat in the yogurt until evenly mixed.

5 Whisk the egg whites in a clean, grease-free bowl until stiff, then fold into the mixture. Divide among the pastry shells and let set.

6 Drizzle the melted chocolate over the tartlets to decorate.

CHOCOLATE PAVLOVA WITH PASSION FRUIT CREAM

4 egg whites

1 cup superfine sugar

4 teaspoons cornstarch

3 tablespoons unsweetened cocoa

1 teaspoon vinegar

chocolate leaves, to decorate

For the filling

5 ounces semisweet chocolate, broken into squares

1 cup heavy or whipping cream

⅔ cup strained plain yogurt

½ teaspoon vanilla extract

4 passion fruit

⌒ SERVES 6 ⌒

Passion fruit is aptly named. Serve this superb sweet and anything could happen!

3 Spread the mixture over the marked circle, making a slight hollow in the center. Bake for 1½-2 hours.

1 Preheat the oven to 275°F. Cut a piece of baking parchment or wax paper to fit a baking sheet. Draw a 9-inch circle on the paper and place the paper upside-down on the baking sheet.

2 Whisk the egg whites in a clean, grease-free bowl until stiff. Gradually whisk in the sugar and continue to whisk until the mixture is stiff again. Whisk in the cornstarch, cocoa and vinegar.

4 Make the filling. Melt the chocolate in a heat proof bowl over hot water, then remove from the heat and cool slightly. In a separate bowl, whip the cream with the yogurt and vanilla extract until thick. Fold 4 tablespoons into the chocolate, then set both mixtures aside.

5 Halve all the passion fruit and scoop out the pulp. Stir half into the plain cream mixture. Carefully remove the meringue shell from the baking sheet and place it on a large serving plate. Fill with the passion fruit cream, then spoon over the chocolate mixture and the remaining passion fruit.

6 Decorate with chocolate leaves before serving.

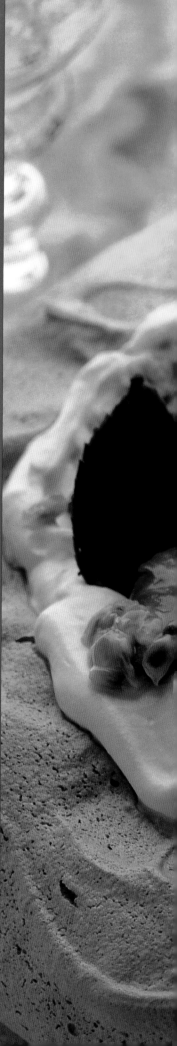

MISSISSIPPI MUD PIE

Mud, mud, glorious mud – isn't that what the song says? Well, you can't get much more glorious than this!

INGREDIENTS

2¼ cups all-purpose flour

⅔ cup unsalted butter

2 egg yolks

1-2 tablespoons ice water

For the filling

3 eggs, separated

4 teaspoons cornstarch

⅓ cup light brown sugar

1¾ cups milk

5 ounces semisweet chocolate, broken into squares

1 teaspoon vanilla extract

1 packet powdered gelatin

3 tablespoons water

2 teaspoons dark rum

For the topping

¾ cup heavy or whipping cream

chocolate curls

~ SERVES 6–8 ~

1 Sift the flour into a bowl and cut in the butter until the mixture resembles coarse breadcrumbs. Stir in the egg yolks with just enough ice water to bind the mixture into a soft dough. Roll out on a lightly floured surface and place in a deep 9-inch tart pan. Chill for about 30 minutes.

2 Preheat the oven to 375°F. Prick the pastry shell all over with a fork, cover with greaseproof paper weighed down with dried beans and bake for 10 minutes. Remove the dried beans and paper, return the pastry shell to the oven and bake for a further 10 minutes, until the pastry is crisp and golden. Cool the pastry shell in the tin.

3 Make the filling. Mix the egg yolks, cornstarch and 2 tablespoons of the sugar in a bowl. Heat the milk in a saucepan until almost boiling, then beat it into the egg mixture. Return to the clean pan and stir over a low heat until the custard has thickened and is smooth. Pour half the custard into a bowl.

4 Melt the chocolate in a heat proof bowl over hot water, then stir into the custard in the bowl, with the vanilla extract. Spread in the pastry shell, cover with plastic wrap to prevent from forming a skin, cool, then chill until set.

5 Sprinkle the gelatin over the water in a small bowl, let sit until spongy, then place over simmering water until all the gelatine has dissolved. Stir into the remaining custard, with the rum. Whisk the egg whites in a clean, grease-free bowl until stiff peaks form, whisk in the remaining sugar, then fold quickly into the custard before it sets.

6 Spoon the mixture over the chocolate custard to cover completely. Chill until set, then remove the pie from the pan and place on a serving plate. Spread whipped cream over the top and sprinkle with chocolate curls.

MANGO AND CHOCOLATE CREME BRULEE

INGREDIENTS

2 ripe mangoes

1¼ cups heavy or whipping cream

1¼ cups crème fraîche

1 vanilla bean

4 ounces bittersweet chocolate, broken into squares

4 egg yolks

1 tablespoon honey

6 tablespoons raw sugar, for topping

~ SERVES 6 ~

1 Peel, halve, and pit the mangoes. Roughly chop the flesh and divide it among six ovenproof ramekins set on a baking sheet.

2 Mix the cream and crème fraîche in a large heat proof bowl and add the vanilla bean. Place the bowl over a saucepan of barely simmering water and stir for about 10 minutes. Do not let the bowl touch the water or the cream may overheat.

Pure luxury – exotic fruit in a honeyed chocolate custard, topped with a crunchy coating of caramelized sugar.

3 Remove the vanilla bean and stir in the chocolate, a few pieces at a time, until melted. When the mixture is completely smooth, remove the bowl, but leave the pan of water over the heat.

4 Whisk the egg yolks and honey in a second heat proof bowl, then gradually pour in the chocolate cream, whisking constantly. Place over the pan of simmering water and stir constantly until the chocolate custard thickens enough to coat the back of a wooden spoon.

5 Remove from the heat and spoon the custard over the mangoes. Cool, then chill in the fridge until set.

6 Preheat the broiler to high. Sprinkle 1 tablespoon raw sugar evenly over each dessert and spray lightly with a little water. Broil briefly, as close to the heat as possible, until the sugar melts and caramelizes. Chill the desserts before serving once more.

COOK'S TIP

The mango and chocolate custard base can be prepared up to two days in advance. Make the caramelized sugar topping several hours before serving so that the desserts can be chilled.

CHOCOLATE HAZELNUT GALETTES

There are stacks of sophistication in these triple-tiered chocolate rounds sandwiched with a light ricotta filling.

INGREDIENTS

6 ounces semisweet chocolate, broken into squares

3 tablespoons cream

2 tablespoons slivered hazelnuts

4 ounces white chocolate, broken into squares

¾ cup ricotta cheese

1 tablespoon dry sherry

4 tablespoons finely chopped hazelnuts, toasted

raspberries, dipped in white chocolate, to decorate

SERVES 4

1 Melt the semisweet chocolate in a heat proof bowl over hot water, remove from heat and stir in cream.

2 Draw sixteen 3-inch circles on sheets of baking parchment or wax paper. Turn the paper over and spread the plain chocolate over each circle, covering in a thin, even layer. Sprinkle slivered hazelnuts over four of the circles, then leave until set.

3 Melt the white chocolate in a heat proof bowl over a pan of hot water, then stir in the ricotta and dry sherry. Fold in the chopped, toasted hazelnuts. Let cool until the mixture is firm.

4 Remove the twelve plain chocolate rounds carefully from the paper and sandwich them in stacks of three, spooning the white chocolate hazelnut cream between each layer and topping them with the four hazelnut-covered rounds. Chill before serving.

5 To serve, place the galettes on individual plates and decorate with white chocolate–dipped raspberries.

COOK'S TIP

The chocolate could be spread over heart shapes instead, for a special Valentine's Day dessert.

139

$\mathscr{S}$WEETS AND DRINKS

Chocolate truffles, nutty fudge and liqueur-spiked filled chocolates and candies are simple and rewarding to make, and packed into pretty boxes they make wonderful gifts. For after-dinner sweet treats, Cognac and Ginger Creams or Peppermint Chocolate Sticks are so much more special than bought mints. If you prefer chocolate drinks, at the end of the day you can sink into a comfy armchair with a warming glass of Irish Chocolate Velvet or Mexican Hot Chocolate.

CHOCOLATE AND CHERRY DELIGHTS

INGREDIENTS

4 ounces bittersweet chocolate, broken into squares

3 ounces white or milk chocolate, broken into squares

2 tablespoons unsalted butter, melted

1 tablespoon Kirsch or brandy

4 tablespoons heavy cream

18-20 maraschino cherries or liqueur-soaked cherries

milk chocolate curls, to decorate

~ MAKES 18–20 ~

For a sweet surprise for a friend or lover, pack these pretty little sweets in a decorative box.

3 Place one cherry in each chocolate case. Spoon the chocolate cream mixture into a piping bag fitted with a small star tip and pipe over the cherries, mounding it in generous swirls.

4 Top each colette with a chocolate curl. Leave until set, then chill in the fridge until needed.

COOK'S TIP

If foil sweet cases are difficult to obtain, use double thickness paper sweet cases instead.

1 Melt the bittersweet chocolate in a bowl over hot water, then remove from the heat. Spoon into 18-20 foil candy cups, spread evenly with a small brush, then leave in a cool place to set.

2 Melt the white or milk chocolate with the butter in a heat proof bowl over hot water. Remove from the heat and stir in the Kirsch or brandy, then the cream. Cool until the mixture is thick enough to hold its shape.

COGNAC AND GINGER CREAMS

Only you know the secret of these handsome hand-made chocolates: that the mysterious dark exterior conceals a glorious ginger and cognac cream filling.

INGREDIENTS

11 ounces bittersweet chocolate, broken into squares

3 tablespoons heavy or whipping cream

2 tablespoons cognac

1 tablespoon preserved ginger syrup

4 pieces of preserved ginger, finely chopped

crystallized ginger, to decorate

MAKES 18-20

1 Polish the insides of about 18-20 chocolate molds with a soft cloth. Melt about two-thirds of the chocolate in a heat proof bowl over hot water, then spoon a little into each mold. Reserve a little of the melted chocolate for sealing the creams.

2 Using a small brush, paint the chocolate up the sides of the molds to coat them evenly, then invert them onto a sheet of wax paper and let set.

3 Melt the remaining chocolate, then stir in the cream, cognac, ginger syrup and ginger, mixing well. Spoon into the chocolate-lined molds. Warm the reserved chocolate if necessary, then spoon a little into each mold to seal. Leave in a cool place (not the fridge) until set.

4 To remove the chocolates from the molds, gently press them out onto a cool surface. Decorate with small pieces of crystallized ginger.

COOK'S TIP

Simple chocolate molds can be bought in most good kitchen stores and give a highly professional finish. Polishing the molds thoroughly with a soft cotton cloth results in really glossy chocolates that are relatively easy to remove. If they do stick, put them in the fridge for a short time, then try again. Don't chill them for too long, or you may dull the surface of the chocolate.

CHOCOLATE FONDANT HEARTS

Get set to impress your love with these luscious hearts. For added romance, pipe both sets of your initials on each.

INGREDIENTS

4 tablespoons liquid glucose

2 ounces bittersweet chocolate, broken into squares

2 ounces white chocolate, broken into squares

1 egg white, lightly beaten

3½ cups confectioners' sugar, sifted

melted dark and white chocolate, to decorate

MAKES ABOUT 50

1 Divide the glucose
~ between two heat proof bowls. Place each bowl over hot water and heat the glucose gently, then add the dark chocolate to one bowl and the white chocolate to the other. Let stand until the chocolate has completely melted.

2 Remove both bowls from
~ the heat and cool slightly. Add half the egg white to each bowl, then divide the confectioners' sugar between them, mixing to combine well.

3 Knead each mixture
~ separately with your hands until smooth and pliable. On a surface lightly dusted with confectioners' sugar, roll out both mixtures separately to a thickness of about ⅛ inch.

4 Brush the surface of the
~ dark chocolate fondant with egg white and place the white chocolate fondant on top. Roll the surface lightly with a rolling pin to press the layers together.

5 Using a small heart-shaped
~ cutter, cut out about 50 hearts from the fondant. Drizzle melted chocolate over each heart to decorate, and chill until firm.

COOK'S TIP

Don't throw away the fondant trimmings – knead them together to create a marbled effect, roll the fondant out again and cut out more hearts or other shapes to use as cake decorations.

MALT WHISKEY TRUFFLES

These tempting truffles make perfect presents – if you can part with them.

INGREDIENTS

7 ounces bittersweet chocolate, broken into squares

⅔ cup heavy or whipping cream

3 tablespoons malt whiskey

1 cup confectioners' sugar

unsweetened cocoa, for coating

⌇ MAKES 25–30 ⌇

1 Melt the chocolate in a heat proof bowl over hot water, then cool slightly.

2 Whip the cream with the whiskey in a bowl until soft peaks form.

3 Fold in the chocolate and confectioners' sugar, mixing evenly, then chill until firm enough to handle.

4 Dust your hands with cocoa and shape the mixture into bite-size balls. Coat in cocoa and pack into pretty boxes. Store in the fridge for up to 3–4 days, if not using immediately.

CHOCOLATE ALMOND TRIANGLES

> ## *Serve this speciality in thin slices.*

INGREDIENTS

4 ounces semisweet chocolate, broken into squares

4 tablespoons unsalted butter

1 egg white

½ cup superfine sugar

½ cup ground almonds

½ cup chopped toasted almonds

5 tablespoons chopped lemon candied peel

For the coating

6 ounces white chocolate, broken into squares

2 tablespoons unsalted butter

1 cup slivered almonds, toasted

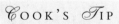

MAKES ABOUT 20 SLICES

COOK'S TIP

The mixture can be shaped into a simple round roll instead of the triangular shape if you prefer.

1 Melt the chocolate with the butter in a heat proof bowl over barely simmering water until smooth.

2 In a clean, grease-free bowl, whisk the egg white with the sugar until stiff. Gradually beat in the melted chocolate, then stir in the ground almonds, toasted almonds and lemon peel.

3 Pour the mixture onto a large sheet of baking parchment or wax paper and shape into a thick roll.

4 As the mixture cools, use the paper to press the roll firmly into a triangular shape. Twist the paper over the triangular roll and chill until completely set.

5 Make the coating. Melt the white chocolate with the butter in a heat proof bowl over hot water. Unwrap the chocolate roll and spread the white chocolate quickly over the surface. Press the almonds in a thin even coating over the chocolate, working quickly before the chocolate sets.

6 Chill again until firm, then cut the triangular roll into fairly thin slices to serve.

RICH CHOCOLATE PISTACHIO FUDGE

INGREDIENTS

1 cup granulated sugar

1 can (13 ounces) sweetened condensed milk

4 tablespoons unsalted butter

1 teaspoon vanilla extract

4 ounces semisweet chocolate, grated

¾ cup pistachios, almonds or hazelnuts

MAKES 36

Make a big batch of this meltingly rich chocolate fudge packed with pistachios — it won't last long!

1 Grease an 8-inch square
~ cake pan and line with baking parchment or wax paper. Mix the sugar, condensed milk and butter in a heavy saucepan. Heat gently, stirring occasionally, until the sugar has dissolved completely.

2 Bring the mixture to a
~ boil, stirring occasionally, and boil until it registers 240°F on a candy thermometer (see Cook's Tip).

3 Remove the pan from the
~ heat and beat in the vanilla extract, chocolate and nuts. Beat vigorously until the mixture is smooth and creamy.

4 Pour the mixture into the
~ prepared cake pan and spread evenly. Leave until just set, then mark into squares. Let mixture set completely before cutting into squares and removing from the pan. Store in an airtight container in a cool place.

COOK'S TIP

If you haven't got a candy thermometer, test the mixture by dropping a small spoonful into a cup of iced water. If you can roll the mixture into a soft ball with your fingertips, the fudge is ready.

CHOCOLATE-COATED NUT BRITTLE

Take equal amounts of pecans and almonds, set them in crisp caramel, then add a dark chocolate coating for a sweet sensation.

INGREDIENTS

1 cup mixed whole pecans and almonds

½ cup superfine sugar

4 tablespoons water

7 ounces bittersweet chocolate, broken into squares

~ MAKES 20–24 PIECES ~

1 Lightly grease a baking
~ sheet with butter or oil.
Mix the nuts, sugar and water
in a heavy saucepan. Place the
pan over low heat, stirring
without boiling until the sugar
has dissolved.

2 Bring to a boil, then lower
~ the heat and cook until the
mixture turns a rich golden
brown and registers 300°F on
a candy thermometer. To test
without a thermometer, drop a
few drops of the mixture into a
cup of iced water. The mixture
should become brittle.

3 Quickly remove the pan
~ from the heat and tip the
mixture onto the prepared
baking sheet, spreading it
evenly. Allow to become
completely cold and hard.

4 Break the nut brittle into
~ bite-size pieces. Melt the
chocolate in a heat proof bowl
over hot water and dip the
pieces to half-coat them. Leave
on a sheet of non-stick baking
paper to set.

COOK'S TIP

These look best in rough chunks, so don't worry if the pieces break unevenly or if there are gaps in the chocolate coating.

PEPPERMINT CHOCOLATE STICKS

Turn the lights down low, curl up on the couch and pamper yourself with these delicious bite-size chocolate sticks.

INGREDIENTS

½ cup granulated sugar

⅔ cup water

½ teaspoon peppermint extract

7 ounces semisweet chocolate, broken into squares

4 tablespoons toasted shredded coconut

MAKES ABOUT 80

1 Lightly grease a large baking sheet. Place the sugar and water in a small heavy saucepan and heat gently, stirring occasionally, until the sugar has dissolved.

2 Bring to a rapid boil and boil without stirring until the syrup registers 280°F on a candy thermometer. Remove the pan from the heat and add the peppermint extract, then pour onto the greased baking sheet and refrigerate until hardened.

3 Break up the peppermint mixture into a small bowl and use the end of a rolling pin to crush it into small pieces.

4 Melt the chocolate in a heat proof bowl over hot water. Remove from the heat and stir in the mint pieces and shredded coconut.

5 Lay a 10 x 12 inch sheet of baking parchment or wax paper on a flat surface. Spread the chocolate mixture over the paper, leaving a narrow border all around, to make a rectangle measuring about 8 x 10 inches. Let set. When firm, use a sharp knife to cut into thin sticks, each about 2½ inches long.

COOK'S TIP

The chocolate mixture could be cut into squares instead, eaten as is, or used as decoration.

MEXICAN HOT CHOCOLATE

Snuggle down in bed with a big mug of spicy hot chocolate. In Mexico, this drink is traditionally whisked with a carved wooden beater called a molinillo, but a modern blender works just as well.

INGREDIENTS

4 cups milk

1 cinnamon stick

2 whole cloves

4 ounces semisweet chocolate, broken into squares

2-3 drops of almond extract

~ SERVES 4 ~

1 ~ Heat the milk gently with the spices in a saucepan until almost boiling, then stir in the chocolate over medium heat until melted.

2 ~ Strain into a blender, add the almond extract and blend on high speed for about 30 seconds until frothy. Alternatively, blend the mixture with a hand-held electric mixer or a wire whisk.

3 ~ Pour into mugs and serve immediately.

COOK'S TIP

If you don't have whole cinnamon and cloves, add a pinch of each of the ground spices to the mixture before whisking.

IRISH CHOCOLATE VELVET

Warm the cockles of your heart with this smooth, sophisticated drink.

INGREDIENTS

½ cup heavy or whipping cream

1¾ cups milk

4 ounces milk chocolate, broken into squares

2 tablespoons unsweetened cocoa

4 tablespoons Irish whiskey

whipped cream, for topping

chocolate curls, to decorate

~ SERVES 4 ~

1 Whip the cream in a bowl ~ until it is thick enough to form stiff peaks.

2 Place the milk and ~ chocolate in a saucepan and heat gently, stirring, until the chocolate has melted.

3 Whisk in the cocoa, then ~ bring to the boil, remove from the heat and add the cream and Irish whiskey.

4 Pour quickly into four ~ mugs or tall glasses and top each serving with a generous spoonful of whipped cream. Decorate with chocolate curls and serve.

COOK'S TIP

If Irish whiskey is not available, use Scotch whisky, brandy or a liqueur based on either.

*I*CED MINT AND CHOCOLATE COOLER

> *Many chocolate drinks are warm and comforting, but this one is really refreshing, ideal for a hot summer's day.*

INGREDIENTS

4 tablespoons hot cocoa mix

1¾ cups cold milk

⅔ cup plain yogurt

½ teaspoon peppermint extract

4 scoops chocolate ice cream

mint leaves and chocolate shapes, to decorate

SERVES 4

1 Place the hot cocoa mix in ~ a small saucepan and stir in about ½ cup of the milk. Heat gently, and stir until the milk is almost boiling, then remove from the heat.

2 Pour into a cold mixing ~ bowl and whisk in the remaining milk, yogurt and peppermint extract.

3 Pour the mixture into four ~ tall glasses and top each with a scoop of ice cream. Decorate with mint leaves and chocolate shapes. Serve immediately.

COOK'S TIP

Use unsweetened cocoa instead of hot cocoa mix if you prefer, but add sugar to taste.

153

$\mathcal{B}$ASIC RECIPES

Chocolate Ganache

A luxurious, creamy frosting for cakes and desserts.

MAKES ENOUGH TO COVER A 9-INCH ROUND CAKE

1 cup heavy or whipping cream
8 ounces semisweet chocolate, broken into squares

1 Heat the cream and chocolate together in a saucepan over low heat, stirring frequently until the chocolate has melted. Pour into a bowl, let cool, then whisk until the mixture begins to stiffen.

Chocolate Buttercream

A quick, everyday filling and frosting.

ENOUGH TO FILL AN 8-INCH ROUND CAKE

6 tablespoons unsalted butter or margarine, softened
1½ cups confectioners' sugar
1 tablespoon unsweetened cocoa
½ teaspoon vanilla extract

1 Place all the ingredients in a large bowl.

2 Beat well to a smooth, spreadable consistency.

White Chocolate Frosting

A fluffy, rich, white frosting for cakes and desserts.

MAKES ENOUGH TO COVER AN 8-INCH ROUND CAKE

6 ounces white chocolate, broken into squares
6 tablespoons unsalted butter
1 cup confectioners' sugar
6 tablespoons heavy or whipping cream

1 Melt the chocolate with the butter in a heat proof bowl over hot water. Remove from the heat and beat in the confectioners' sugar.

2 Whip the cream in a separate bowl until it just holds its shape, then beat into the chocolate mixture. Allow the mixture to cool, stirring occasionally, until it begins to stiffen. Use frosting immediately.

$\mathcal{V}$ARIATION

For a special occasion cake, stir in a tablespoon of brandy or your favorite liqueur.

Glossy Chocolate Sauce

Delicious poured over ice cream or on hot or cold desserts.

SERVES 6

½ cup superfine sugar

4 tablespoons water

6 ounces bittersweet chocolate, broken into squares

2 tablespoons unsalted butter

2 tablespoons brandy or orange juice

1 Place the sugar and water in a saucepan and heat gently, stirring occasionally until the sugar has dissolved.

2 Stir in the chocolate a few squares at a time until melted, then add the butter in the same way. Do not allow the sauce to boil. Stir in the brandy or orange juice and serve warm.

COOK'S TIP

This sauce freezes well. Pour into a freezer-proof container, seal, label and freeze for up to 3 months. Thaw at room temperature.

Chocolate Fondant

Easily molded, this icing gives a smooth finish to celebration cakes, and can also be made into flowers, shapes or cut-outs for decoration.

MAKES ENOUGH TO COVER AND DECORATE
A 9-INCH ROUND CAKE

12 ounces unsweetened chocolate, broken into squares

4 tablespoons liquid glucose

2 egg whites

7 cups confectioners' sugar

1 Melt the chocolate with the glucose in a heat proof bowl over hot water. Stir to mix, remove from the heat and cool slightly.

2 In a clean, grease-free bowl, whisk egg whites lightly, then stir into the chocolate with 3 tablespoons of confectioners' sugar.

3 Using an electric mixer, gradually beat in enough of the remaining confectioners' sugar to make a stiff paste. Cover with plastic wrap if not using immediately.

White Chocolate Sauce

Rich and sweet, this makes a lovely contrast to a bittersweet chocolate mousse or pudding.

SERVES 6
⅔ cup heavy or whipping cream
5 ounces white chocolate, broken into squares
2 tablespoons brandy or Cointreau

1 Pour the cream into a saucepan and heat it gently over low heat until almost boiling. Stir the cream occasionally.

2 Stir in the chocolate, a few squares at a time, until melted and smooth. Remove from the heat and stir in the brandy or Cointreau just before serving.

VARIATIONS

WHITE MOCHA SAUCE: *Stir in 2 tablespoons strong black coffee just before serving.*
COCONUT CHOCOLATE CREAM SAUCE: *Stir in 3 tablespoons powdered coconut just before serving.*

Chocolate Shortcrust Pastry

A rich, dark, chocolate-flavored pastry for sweet custards and tarts.

4 ounces semisweet chocolate, broken into squares
2 cups all-purpose flour
½ cup unsalted butter
1-2 tablespoons cold water

1 Melt the chocolate in a heat proof bowl over hot water. Allow to cool but not set.

2 Place the flour in a mixing bowl. Cut in the butter until the mixture resembles fine bread crumbs.

3 Make a well in the center of the mixture. Add the cooled chocolate, with just enough cold water to mix to a firm dough.

Chocolate Shortcrust Pastry (2)

An alternate chocolate pastry, made with cocoa instead of chocolate.

1½ cups all-purpose flour
2 tablespoons unsweetened cocoa
2 tablespoons confectioners' sugar
½ cup butter
1-2 tablespoons cold water

1 Sift together the flour, cocoa and confectioners' sugar into a bowl.

2 Place the butter in a pan with the water and heat gently until just melted. Cool.

3 Stir into the flour to make a smooth dough. Chill until firm, then roll out and use as required.

Chocolate Baskets or Cups

These impressive baskets make pretty, edible containers for mousse or ice cream.

MAKES 6
6 ounces dark, milk or white chocolate
2 tablespoons butter

1 Cut out six 6-inch circles from baking parchment or wax paper.

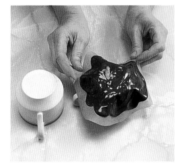

2 Melt the chocolate with the butter in a heat proof bowl over barely simmering water. Stir until smooth. Spoon one-sixth of the chocolate over each circle, using a teaspoon to spread it to within ¾ inch of the edge.

3 Carefully lift each covered paper circle and drape it over an upturned cup or ramekin, curving the edges to create a frilled effect.

4 Leave until completely set, then carefully lift off the chocolate circle and peel away the paper.

5 For a different effect, brush the chocolate over, leaving the edges jagged.

Chocolate-dipped Fruit

Strawberries, grapes, cherries and other small fruits taste absolutely delicious when fully or partially coated in chocolate, as do mandarin segments. Fruit for dipping should be ripe but not soft, and clean and dry. Whole nuts such as almonds or brazil nuts can also be dipped.

1 Melt some chocolate and remove from the heat. Dip the fruits or nuts fully or halfway into the chocolate and allow the excess to drip off.

2 Place the fruit on a baking sheet lined with waxed paper and chill until completely set.

Chocolate Squiggles

Melt some chocolate and spread fairly thinly over a cool, smooth surface. Leave until just set, then draw a citrus zester firmly across the surface to remove curls or "squiggles" of the chocolate.

$\mathscr{I}$NDEX

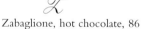